The Mystery of Miracles

Beatrice Schuller

Visit my website at www.beatriceschuller.com

Printed in the United States of America

First Printing 2014
By
Sojourn Publishing, LLC

ISBN: 978-1-62747-060-5
Ebook ISBN: 978-1-62747-061-2
LCN: Pending

Table of Contents

Dedication

This book is dedicated to my maternal grandmother, Emma Billings, who lived a life of unconditional love. She was a femme sole business owner at a time when it was not easy to succeed, especially as a dairy farmer and then cattle rancher. She filled her home with grace and laughter, never having a harsh word for anyone.

Grandmother, thank you for inspiring me to seek out peace, love, and a fulfilled life, attributes that led me to the Divine. I sought after and found that inner joy that bubbled out of you all your life. I am eternally grateful.

Acknowledgements

I acknowledge with a joyful heart:

Author Brad Cullen and his publisher Ryan Bruce for their spirit filled and timely insight.

Michael Mirdad and Dr. Wayne Dyer for their teachings and books.

Tom Bird's Sojourn Publishing for the training method that connects even the novice writer to the Divine Author within. I am eternally grateful dear Tom and Rama.

Many friends have played a role in the creation of this book:
  Bob Burnside who encouraged and supported me to take serious steps toward becoming an author. Roxanne Miller who gently led me into the

metaphysical world of possibilities. Many others include: Ann Kelton, Shaheena Ausaf, Jean Gray, Amanda Romania and Pat and Dick Bridgforth.

My beloved John is a big fan and supporter of my writing, along with my sons Norman, Bert and Troy.

Thank you all for your unconditional love and encouragement.

Introduction

I wrote this book for you. No matter what nationality you may be, sect, religion, or culture, this book reveals the mysteries behind miracles and their components so you can seek out and facilitate miracles in your own life and the lives of others.

I have shared some personal events from my private life in an effort to demonstrate the reality of this fact, for it is not just a pipe dream. You really can facilitate miracles of health, wealth, and happiness as long as it originates from the divine power within yourself.

The first thirty years of my life were quite a mess, as I did not bother to access the Divine. Like many others, I was at the mercy of my circumstances and my bad decisions. Then in 1974, in a desperate situation, I cried out for help—just in case there was a real God out there somewhere. As a result, I became aware of this reunited force within me in a dramatic and supernatural way, and so began my transformation. I still made some bad choices on occasion, but now I could access a power beyond my own human ability and intellect. I had a go-to source and received direction and miraculous aid in various forms. I was rescued from many a crisis generated by others and sometimes my own actions. Eventually, I learned how to make better decisions. This life-changing encounter and subsequent spiritual growth all happened outside any church or religion. Later when I delved into main stream Christianity and other religions, I found wonderful friends and fellowship. It was a welcome environment for my spiritual growth. Sermons and teachings were built around supernatural events recorded in Bibles and texts, but I heard no one declaring that we should expect to experience these things today. It was all for the "by and by" if we proved ourselves to be "worthy" in this life. I was not about to start rejecting the joy and blessings I had found in order to conform to the religious community. So I continued my journey with this God of Unconditional Love who guided me through original translations of Holy Scripture, along with a cache of books and texts that led to my spiritual growth and understanding.

Eventually, I was compelled to unravel what seemed such a mystery to me. Why did most religions and sects hold to the doctrine of an unforgiving and vengeful deity that would torture/kill the very people the deity had created? How could even a loving *human* Father do that to his own offspring?

I was beginning to understand another enigma that had always puzzled me. Why do nations continue with wars in which we send our young and healthy to kill one another? There are other solutions to conflicts. Something was obviously amiss in our perception of what a Worshipful God would sanction. By searching through original writings by early Christian teachers from the second century, I began to understand how present-day religious doctrines evolved. The true God of Unconditional Love had been written out of historical Biblical accounts and replaced with a God of Vengeance who ordered mass killings of unbelievers.

The Christian masses have been reading from mistranslations of the original Biblical writings, beginning with the first printed version of the King James Bible in 1611. These insidious doctrines are still taught in seminaries today and embraced by their religious converts. In this book, you will discover the true translation of key scriptures written and preserved by those who experienced personal encounters thousands of years ago. Because the Creator of All is known by many different names, please understand that I am in effect referring to "God, by any other title or name given by people of different nations and cultures." I hope you can consider our Creator as eternally present. We as human souls for the most part have lived as if we are separate from the Divine. Our perception of God has evolved through time as we awaken and gain understanding through scientific confirmations of Divine influence in which we share in creation. We are beginning to create good instead instead of bad, because we do indeed create as long as we are living on this Earth.

There are certain common components involved in facilitating miracles brought about by our Creator. They neither have anything to do with doctrines, nor do they depend upon religious rituals. It is important that I share some of my personal failures with you as well as the victories. One of the mysteries behind miracles is how they occur to ordinary people, even unbelievers living contrary to any pious lifestyle. If this is a new concept for you, it is my hope to convince you that miracles *can* occur to every one of us in our daily lives. With this understanding and applied components, you can improve your life and the lives of others.

Let us set aside any differences perpetuated by religions and sects that tend to separate us from God and from one another. By whatever name or label these organized religions use, they have set up rituals and certain practices in their effort to make us acceptable to their brand of God.

My life of miracles is a result of awakening to the fact that we are all connected to our Creator and thereby to one another. Religions may serve to enrich our lives on some levels, but they do not take the place of knowing and acting upon the reality of this personal connection and alignment with a God of Unconditional Love.

With this in mind, I invite you to read my story.

Chapter 1

Check It Out Yourself

Bless those who challenge us to grow, to stretch, to move beyond the knowable, to come back home to our elemental and essential nature. Bless those who challenge us, for they remind us of doors we have closed and doors we have yet to open.

~ Navajo saying

In the last few decades, there has been such a scarcity of publicized miracles that we laugh at the excitement generated over a tortilla having a likeness of the Virgin Mary. I recall seeing a TV reporter showing an image of a flour tortilla with what some considered a burned image of the Virgin Mary. The tortilla was being auctioned on eBay for hundreds of dollars. But real miracles are on the rise as more and more people discover that Divine

1

spark within that connects them to the Source of All and to one another. Religions and sects have inadvertently propagated the idea that we remain separate from God, with no means of making a connection with the immortal one until after we die. To further widen the breach, organized religion demands certain rules and rituals be practiced to attain that heavenly place and avoid eternal separation and torment. There are varying degrees of this doctrine taught in the world's religions, but basically that is the general theme.

No matter which of these religions you may embrace, a mistranslation of vital words like *sin, salvation,* and *believe* will distort the truth of what was actually penned in the Greek language thousands of years ago.

The Greek word for *sin* means to "miss the bull's eye on a target." This alone shatters the doctrine that a "Just God" would send sinners to Hell. The truth is we all sin over and over again through our carnal natures, thus creating hellish situations in various degrees for ourselves and others. Who can live a perfect life? If you believe New Testament accounts of Jesus' life, then you have to believe he lost his temper in his own synagogue, turning over tables and cursing the Pharisees while yielding a whip. Hardly what our priests and pastors call pious behavior. It does serve to remind us that we humans are not perfect specimens of behavior.

Now let's take a look at the Greek meaning of *salvation* before it was erroneously turned into an eternal place far, far away where we can walk on golden streets. Being "saved" actually translates as a *rejoining* or *being reunited.* Of course you can see there first has to be a union before a reunion can occur. This description discredits the commonly accepted idea that our union with God depends upon following religious rules of behavior. We might *choose* to follow rules or rituals, but they truly do not translate into our "salvation" or "reunion" with God. Which takes us to the meaning of the word *believe* in the original Greek, which is: *adhere to, rely on,* and *trust in.*

Translate all of this into the modern world of the twenty-first century and what do we have? The truth is this: If any of us *miss perfection in our daily lives,* but *trust in, rely on, and stick to* the One Source of All, then we can *reunite* or *rejoin* by reconnecting to that Source, the source of redemption and of miracles.

This is truly the "Tidings of great joy which shall be to all people" heralded by the angels at the birth of Jesus 2,000 years ago.[1] Jesus knew at an early age who he was and who we all are. He

_____

[1] Luke 2:10

3

taught this universal message to thousands of open and receptive hearts.

Unfortunately, he was rejected by his own people. The miraculous supernatural events facilitated by Jesus have been recorded for us as a pattern we can all follow. Instead of the distorted messages concerning these major truths, we can take Jesus at his word and live a life of miracles.

His words that I took to heart forty years ago were: "If you believe me, you can do the same things I do and even greater."[2] I did believe what he said and I did trust and obey. You have that choice as well.

An interesting side note for this subject concerns a reference I found while researching early religions online. It seems the Muslim faith was taken from early writings from the Bible. "They [Muslims] believe that Islam is the complete and universal version of a primordial faith that has been revealed before through many prophets including Abraham, Moses, Ishmael, and Jesus. Muslims also believe that these previous Islamic messages and revelations have been partially changed or corrupted over time."[3] It seems we are all in the same boat as far as depending on our clergy to lead us into all truth.

---

[2] John 14:21
[3] Wikipedia Online

Today, science is proving the existence of God through quantum theory and other discoveries. Of course, many forget that Einstein with all his intellect knew there was a Universal God of design.[4]

Physicist and author Gregg Braden explains how God's presence is in our life-giving breath and then shared with one another, sustaining all life around us. As we take in oxygen, we breathe out carbon dioxide to sustain the Earth's plant life, which then produces and releases oxygen into the air, creating a beautiful cycle of life.[5]

Because of technological achievements, we can share life-giving information from our own experiences and studies. For example, we can now use timely information to diagnose our health problems and then give our bodies what they need to heal.

Scientific studies of the brain support the existence of our ability to connect with that divine source within as we perceive he/she/it through the intelligence and power of left and right brain, which operates through and beyond the subconscious levels.

This is the scenario for miracles to happen, and I am going to share with you how I learned to facilitate these events and of course, how you can, too.

---

[4] Wikipedia-Einstein's Universal God
[5] Gregg Braden, *The Science of Miracles*

Chapter 2

A Many-Membered Miracle

"There are only two ways to live your life. One is as though nothing is a miracle. The other is as though everything is a miracle."

~ Albert Einstein

I think Einstein would have been proud to join the eight people involved in the following miracle that took place in my home in the early eighties. We had moved to north Houston in a beautiful bedroom community. I had my dream house—a two-story Tudor—and wanted to live the American dream with my three teenage sons and my husband, a naval architect.

My plan took root when I dragged us all to a little Methodist chapel in a nearby town. Our first time ever to visit a church and it was like herding cats. Of course we arrived late. In spite of that, I saw a lot of empty pews, and those occupied seemed to be filled with mostly senior citizens. I almost laughed upon seeing all those white and gray heads of hair.

I steered my crew toward a set of stairs to our right. We all gave a sigh of relief to discover an inviting dark balcony overlooking the sanctuary. My sons looked around and soon were smiling. It seemed this was the hideout for teenagers, including some good-looking girls. We settled in and listened as a parishioner read a short passage from the Bible and then the congregation sang a song from the hymnal—every single verse. We all mouthed the words as best we could to the unknown melody. Then the soft-spoken pastor took to the podium and gave us a precise twenty-minute sermon punctuated by funny little jokes. The offering took place, we sang a final song, and, before we knew it, we were on our way back home to a roast in the oven and a football game on TV. It was a match made in heaven. Little did I know that four years later, I would be teaching Sunday School and holding prayer workshops in our newly built sanctuary where Pastor held three Sunday services.

It was about that time that the miracle occurred in our home. There was still no official prayer chain set up at the church. Methodists are big into fellowship but not too focused on prayer, so I took it upon myself to host a prayer group every Wednesday morning in my home. I had two faithful "prayer partners"—my two best friends, Margie and Beth—who came faithfully every week, as did several other young gals from church. We were a close-knit group and had recently attended a large prayer meeting in Houston at the home of a woman whose book, *Through the Glass Darkly*, we had been reading. She had been dramatically healed of cancer without traditional treatment.

On that Monday before our scheduled prayer meeting, my friend Margie called and told me that she felt led to prepare and bring sacraments for communion to our meeting on Wednesday. She related all the special instructions involving utensils and ingredients in preparing the homemade loaf of bread. Knowing that my friend was a little "out there" anyway, I wasn't too surprised by this until she mentioned she was told to bring wine instead of the grape juice we used at church. I told her I was gong to call Pastor just to let him know what we were doing and get his blessings. In the subsequent call, he told me to do whatever the Lord was leading and added that he had no problem with the wine.

The next day, I received a call from Edith, the church secretary, telling me that a lady had called wanting to get on the prayer chain. She told the lady about our meetings and gave her my address and phone number and just wanted to alert me to the possibility I might hear from her.

On Wednesday when Margie arrived with a bottle of Lancer's red wine, I was a little relieved I had not heard from the "mystery" woman. I had no idea how our own communion service would be done. On the dining room table, we placed the loaf of bread on a silver tray and six of my best crystal goblets.

Later after the girls arrived, we began with the usual time of sharing before prayer. Beth had brought a letter from the Catholic Church her family had left when they moved to Texas from New York. The congregation had been praying for a young boy with an inoperable brain tumor and the boy was now healed. We all joined her with tears of joy as she read from the letter.

Next, another friend opened her Bible to read a passage from I Kings which was an account of Elijah building an altar alongside an altar built to the god of Baal. Miraculously, fire came down and proved Elijah's God was real and powerful. The other gal in our circle interrupted the story to tell us she had been led to read the very same passage. In light of everything that was happening, I shared my thoughts with the group.

"Maybe God is going to do something really big today," I said excitedly.

Next, we discussed all our prayer requests and prepared to enter our customary random prayer time. Just then, the doorbell rang and I excused myself, opened the door to find a woman looking a little flustered and apologizing for being late. "Hello. My name is Cara. I called the church and they gave me directions but I had trouble finding the house. You have a prayer meeting here today?"

I introduced myself and led her into the den to meet the others. When Cara did not have anything to add to our request list, we continued on with our prayers. Although I gave time and waited for a prayer from Cara, she was silent, so I closed the meeting with our traditional, "And so it is."

Beginning to feel anxious about leading the communion service, I told the group how Margie had felt led to bring sacraments, but if anyone needed to leave early, that would be fine. To my chagrin, Cara followed us all into the dining room. As I poured the wine into the glasses, I grew even more nervous as I sat down to lead us in the ritual I had seen performed monthly in our church.

After passing around the plate of bread so we all could take a portion, I said a short prayer about

Christ's body of sacrifice and we all chewed on our delicious bread. I could hardly swallow, but I got mine down. Then I bowed my head to say a prayer about Jesus' blood spilled for our sakes. To my surprise, instead of a prayer, I had a little Jewish-sounding song repeating through my mind. This was something that came during my own private prayer time to kind of "fill in the blanks" between my "speaking" to God. There was no thinking involved and I just let it come forth from my heart it seemed. The shock was that it filled my mind now. I instinctively knew I was being prompted to sing it out aloud, and my body broke into a nervous sweat as I sat trying to make a decision. Would I obey the urging I felt or make up an appropriate prayer? I had never shared my little singing language in front of anyone and didn't carry a tune very well anyway.

After what seemed like an eternity, I succumbed to the prompting of my heart from Spirit and sang out the little song. To my relief, I did not hear a shuffling of feet running to the door. As soon as it stopped, the melody began again but this time the words were in English, and I gratefully sang them out to the same little tune. It was just a verse about how much God loved us. I quickly prayed something about the wine symbolic of Christ's blood and, reluctantly opened my eyes. Thank goodness everyone was still at the table. We all took a good swig of the wine.

Not a word was spoken. It seemed no one—including me—knew where to go from there. Then Cara sat down her goblet and looked around the table.

"I guess you are all wondering why I'm here."

She then explained that she lived about ten miles away and belonged to a Baptist church there. She had been going around to every church she could find to make prayer requests for Kevin, her ten-year-old son. He was suffering from an inoperable brain tumor in the last stages. There was nothing more the doctors could do for his pain other than morphine. The shunt that had been placed in his skull to relieve the pressure was no longer effective and the pain had increased to the point he could not attend school or baseball practice and games with his team. Cara explained that she did not have the faith to believe in the only recourse now for her son—that of God's healing—and so she was seeking the faith of others.

"I know God sometimes heals," she said, 'but most times He does not." Cara looked around at our eyes filling with tears and then Margie spoke to her.

"You need to go see this lady in Houston. God healed her of cancer and...."

Suddenly, I found myself standing up and declaring, "No! God is going to heal your son right now—today." They all looked at me in astonishment. I continued, "Don't you see? God has been building our faith all day—all week actually. You were all given a suggestion. Something was placed on your heart to do and you all did it. Beth, you read the letter about the healing of the boy WITH THE SAME CONDITION."

I turned to Sue and Diane: "Think about the urging of both of you to read the same passage about AN EVENT SHOWING GOD'S FAITHFUL POWER. Then I was challenged to obey the voice within and sing that song about God's love. Margie obeyed the call to bring these sacraments, which she obediently and meticulously prepared. Did it somehow serve to sanctify this whole beautiful event for us in our religious mindset?"

I then asked Cara if she would allow us to pray for her little Kevin in proxy through her and, with a look of wonderment on her face, she said, "Yes."

We gathered around her in her chair and placed our hands on her and prayed for healing for Kevin Afterwards, we joined in a tear-filled time of hugging before the girls began to leave. I told Cara to call me as soon as she got home and she promised to do so.

About an hour later, the phone rang and Cara said cautiously,

"Kevin has no pain, Beatrice."

Tears of joy filled my eyes and then we were both sobbing and thanking God. I asked Cara if she could take him to the doctor but she said they had an appointment in a few days and promised to call me after that visit.

The phone call that came later from her confirmed the healing. The doctor had removed the shunt and because he knew of no explanation, he gave her the only one he could.

"The cancer is in remission," adding, "the medical field has no language for miracles but we see them from time to time."

That would have been the end of the story, except that about a year later, we sold our home and bought property in another county and built another home. I lost touch with Cara. But three years later, I drove back to the Kingwood area to hear a speaker at a large nondenominational church. I was running late, as usual, and arrived to find a full parking lot. Making my way through rows of cars, I saw a lone woman approaching the church from the other side of the parking lot. We arrived at the door together and I was elated to see it was Cara. I thought, *What are the odds?*

We hugged and I asked how little Kevin was doing.

"He's not so little anymore, but he is doing great. He is still into baseball and his team recently won a national division championship." She continued, "The cancer is still in remission, but I worry about it coming back."

I told her the cancer would never come back and to try and relax and enjoy the blessed healing.

I left that church before the speaker finished. As it turned out, my only reason for being there was to be able to share the reality of that wonderful miracle with you and others. God did not just reach out and heal that little boy who was desperately in need of a miracle. We need to ask ourselves why God doesn't just heal everyone all over the planet when they need it. Even the healings of Jesus we have recorded in the Bible demonstrate the same component we have here in this miracle.

One of those incidents involved two blind men coming to Jesus seeking a miracle. Jesus didn't place his hand on their eyes or quote a scripture or tell them to go sacrifice at the temple. That is something they might have willingly done.

No, Jesus bent down in a mud puddle and put some gooey dirt on their eyes and told them to go wash in a certain pool.

A rational mind would ask, "Why would you put faith in some mud on your eyes to bring back your eyesight?" Jesus spoke what He heard from His heart, a heart connected to his Spirit Parent— our Spirit Parent. The men obeyed the instructions and between the three of them, the miracle of restored sight occurred to both men.

Remember Jesus said, "Why do you call me good? Only God the Father is good. The things you see me do is the Father doing them."

In other words, Jesus is explaining he was just facilitating the miracle from God, his Father. Jesus was speaking to a people in a time when this was the traditional understanding of their "Father of Abraham," the Creator of all.

After generations of life experiences, we can move on to understand that Jesus' words and those of other Ascended Masters apply to all mankind no matter how they come to know the Divine. It matters not what route is taken to access that divinity and cocreate with it. What matters is understanding that we are all connected to a God of Unconditional Love.

That Source of love and power and peace is within each of us and when we make a connection, when we are aware of that union, it can result in a miracle for us and others. That miracle for little Kevin evolved around the trusting and then obeying of a thought, a feeling, an urge. Even my left brain logical mind was putting things together that day and, combined with my faith and under-standing of my Spirit Parent, everything came together into a knowing.

As I spoke those words of certainty about Kevin's healing, there was no *hoping* for it, no *wishful thinking* or *maybes* involved. It was a knowing as well as I knew my own name and it came straight from my heart. That is how a miracle can manifest when we choose to facilitate one. That is why it seems so mystical and may seem out of reach for us "down-to-earth" people.

Remember, everyone at my house that day facilitated in this miracle by listening to their inner voices, then acting upon what they heard. You must trust in what and who you are hearing, knowing it is your eternal Creator you are placing your trust in, and then—obey. That is our formula for facilitating a miracle.

Jesus said to be as little children, pure in heart. These are the ones described in the beatitudes[6] in which we are assured, "Blessed are the pure in heart for they shall see God." Jesus also said, "The kingdom of God is within you." A *kingdom* is equivalent to a *realm* or *seat of power* in our present age. These basic concepts will manifest in other miraculous forms as you will learn in the following chapters.

---

[6] Matthew 5 KJV

Chapter 3

ESP or Miracle?

Give thanks for unknown blessings already on their way.
~ Native American Prayer

We have to think with our rational minds to keep jobs and careers going, raising families, and keeping fit and healthy. You may think meditation, miracles, and prayer are for those with time on their hands and no responsibilities. Nothing could be further from the truth.

Miracles happen every day all around us, but most of them go unrecognized as such. So we call little everyday events "coincidences." Yes, these may seem to be "freaky" events, but who is to say we are not creating these things ourselves—on another level of consciousness perhaps.

Another term for this type of event is "extrasensory perception" (ESP), but it definitely does not occur in our left brain rational thinking mode. ESP can be useful in the facilitating of a miracle, along with intuition, and we would do well to embrace it as a spiritual tool. Another term for so-called coincidences is *synchronicity.* I will address this metaphysical term more fully at the end of chapter 4.

Let's look at a good example for recognizing and appreciating all these tools. My late husband, Robert, and I were preparing to drive up to our country home from Houston one Saturday. I was putting on the last touches of makeup when something like a movie ran through my mind. I was inside a car that was swerving all over the highway, missing cars and then veering off the road, heading for a construction site with orange cones and heavy equipment sitting idle in the dirt. The speed of the car and the slamming of the brakes produced a huge cloud of dust all around the car as we slid to a violent stop.

I sat there looking at myself in the mirror wondering what the heck that was all about. I finally concluded it was my vivid imagination having a field day in my brain. I quickly forgot it and realized Robert was waiting for me at the door and we walked out to the car together. I usually drove out to our country place, so Robert went to the passenger side and got in. For some reason, I knocked on his window and said, "Honey, why don't you drive today?" With Robert at the wheel, we headed out to I-45 north of Houston and entered the crowded interstate highway.

Robert and I like to drive in the far left lane and that is where we were when suddenly, a large blue ice chest—the kind you find in a large boat— appeared in front of us. There was nothing to our left except concrete dividers. I watched Robert drive straight into the ice chest. It caught up under the car as he gently applied the brakes and made his way through the cars in the right-hand lanes. All the while, smoke and screeching noises were coming from under the car.

I could hardly believe my eyes as I looked at the construction site that suddenly appeared in front of us. It was exactly as I had seen earlier in my vision. The car bounced around and then came to a sudden stop. We quickly exited the car from a cloud of dirt and there sat the ice chest that had come loose after we hit the dirt. I listened spellbound as Robert explained that had he not caught it between the two front wheels, we would have been catapulted up into the air and into all the traffic. I'm sure if I had been driving I would have instinctively tried to avoid the thing and whipped the wheel to the right, driving up onto the ice chest.

This is one of those mysteries we cannot explain with our finite minds. The more we use our "subconscious and beyond" thinking, the more we will automatically make decisions that protect and prosper us.

Something similar happened one night years earlier while we were actually living full time in our country home. My teenage son was out in our truck one night doing who knows what on a weekend. It was past his curfew and I was awakened by a "dream" of a truck swerving around and eventually slamming into and up over a curbed sidewalk. I got up and went into another room to pray for his safety and then into the kitchen for a drink of water when I heard the truck pull up out front. I met my son at the door and asked him if he was all right. He looked pretty shook up. "What do you mean am I all right?" he asked. I explained to him what I had seen and he told me he had just avoided a collision and had done something to the left tire. We went out to inspect the front wheel that had been bent badly when he swerved up into a high curb to avoid the oncoming car. We had to replace the wheel.

We have here another example of a subtle prompting to intervene in a potentially harmful situation for someone else. This was a simple intervention accomplished by facilitating a "miraculous" solution to a problem. It is your decision whether to take any action, be it prayer or anything else you are prompted to do. Once you become familiar with this divine power within, you will become more and more responsive to these promptings.

Understand that this power within is universal intelligence. If we continuously fail to respond to promptings to facilitate a miracle, then eventually there may be no more promptings. Would you waste time with an exercise in futility? I can assure you the more you respond to these subconscious promptings, the more you will receive them.

.

Chapter 4

Fun-filled Miracles
Can Be Life Changing

If you would be a real seeker after truth, you must at least once in your life doubt, as far as possible, all things.

~ Descartes

In 2003, my dear husband, Robert, passed away after thirty years of marriage. I will have more to add about our marriage and business ventures further along in the book. His sudden death was devastating, and it thrust me into the most challenging time of my life, which you will discover in subsequent chapters.

Several mysterious things happened to me in 2007 after I managed to sell the business in Texas and retire. What appeared to be an ordinary booking of a trip for fun and adventure became a life-changing event for me. A variety of unexplainable things happened on that trip to Yellowstone National Park. These episodes stand as a great example of how intuition and expectation or "faith," if you prefer, can bring about both small and mighty miracles.

I was picked up at the airport by Katie, the tour guide—an energetic, confident, and capable gal—who immediately dispelled any fears or second thoughts I had been nursing about the demands of this all-women adventure tour. I felt entirely safe in this woman's hands. We headed to the cabins in Jackson Hole Wyoming, and I was soon introduced to the other five ladies who would join me on the tour. There was one very nice couple who had been together for twenty years, an FBI employee from the West Coast and another nice single lady from the East Coast.

On the second day as we continued to share and get acquainted, I knew I was being placed in the typical profile for a Southern conservative lady from the Bible belt. The first hint came after questions about my political party, thoughts on abortion, and other ideals that some may use to separate us as Americans. Although my comments were honest and noncondemning, the women continued to challenge me on issues and eventually brought religion into their queries. I actually enjoyed our exchanges, appreciative of hearing their different perspectives on subjects. After two days on the Snake River, we were beginning to bond, and a friendly camaraderie developed among us all, including Katie.

We were on our way back to town to shop when the word "sin" came up in one of their questions. I explained that the word "sin" only meant "missing perfection" and NOT a practice that would send anyone to hell other than one we can make ourselves. I shared with them the original translation that referred to "missing the bull's eye on a target." I was paired up with the FBI gal and she followed me into several stores until I asked what her interests were. She suggested we find a bookstore. Later as we looked through a display of paperbacks, she picked up a book titled *The New Earth* by Eckhart Tolle. She said something like, "If you want to learn something spiritual, you should read this guy." I bought the book. Later after dinner, it was my turn to share a cabin with the tour guide. Katie was reading Al Gore's book on global warming and I was a few chapters into *The New Earth* when I came across a passage I just had to share with Katie. Tolle was explaining the correct translation of the word "hell," and it was almost verbatim to my conversation earlier in the van. Katie responded, "I suppose you are going to share that on the way to Yellowstone tomorrow."

I said, "Well, I think I owe it to them, don't you?" We both laughed, but it got pretty quiet in the van the next day after I shared it with the gals.

None of us had ever visited Yellowstone before and we were filled with anticipation. Katie was telling us she had never seen a grizzly after all these years of leading tours through the park. I told the group that if we all joined our desires and intentions for that to happen, it would increase the chances. "So do we all agree we wish to see a grizzly on our trip to Yellowstone?"

One gal said, "Yes, as long as it is not a personal encounter," and I laughed and agreed she had a good point.

Our subsequent experiences in Yellowstone, according to Katie, were unprecedented. As we rode our bikes from one geyser to the next, they would erupt as if on schedule. This was a first for her to see all of them in one visit. Then we scheduled our viewing of Old Faithful but had to take refuge in a store from a short rain shower. As we emerged, Old Faithful was at it highest and what a surprise we had. We grabbed our cameras to catch a picture of the double rainbow glimmering in the sky over the towering column of water.

I kept saying what a "blessed trip" we were having and it became a joke about "blessed Bea." As we started on the road to exit the park and return to Jackson Hole, a car slowed in front of us and then stopped. We looked to our left and there not thirty feet from the road was a mama grizzly and her two cubs nonchalantly grubbing and grazing. We grabbed our cameras and stood a good while outside the car in awe and so grateful to see such a sight.

Back in the car and talking about next day plans to visit Cascade Canyon, the FBI gal said, "Hey, Bea, can we see a moose tomorrow?"

I answered gleefully, "Let's all put our minds to it and ask to see a moose." Katie let us know that it was not unusual to see a moose at Cascade Canyon. Next day as our little group hiked alone, along the stream that had formed the lake below, we stopped and opened our backpacks to have lunch. Sitting among the rocks, munching and chatting, we looked up the stream to see a moose calmly walking toward us. Whether coincidence or not, it was another blessed day.

The book, *The New Earth*, went home with me, along with a desire to see Sedona, Arizona. Katie had told me she thought Sedona would suit me. Years later, I would visit several times before finally moving to this beautiful place. But before that, I would finish Tolle's book and then listen to an Oprah Winfrey podcast with him. His insight and understanding of our oneness and purpose in life set me further along on my quest for enlightenment and understanding. Consequently, Oprah's show collected emails so that ladies interested in forming discussion groups for the book could find each other.

I connected with three other ladies nearby and we formed our own little study group. We shared our knowledge and understanding and tools for spiritual growth. The Muslim lady from Pakistan is responsible for my developing breathing meditations that took me deeper into areas of my self that needed healing. One of the gals helped me understand and utilize other mysterious tools for spiritual growth and awareness like tarot and pendulums. They told me they were encouraged by the faith I exhibited from my years of trusting the Divine within. We were strengthened by our bond as we made life choices that put us on a path to love, peace, joy, and abundance.

Yes, mysterious, unexplainable things happened on that trip to Yellowstone, but it did not end there. I have since written a screenplay based on three women who discovered they had taken different routes but arrived at the same destination to find a God of Unconditional Love. I am looking to connect with a studio that will produce this inspiring movie so that multitudes may seek out and find the blessings we ladies now enjoy.

Chapter 5

Look Out
For The Blessings

Your task is not to seek for love, but merely to seek and find all the barriers within yourself that you have built against it.

~ Rumi

In 2008, I bought a house and settled down in an active adult community outside of Houston to be near my family. I enjoyed bonding with my children, daughters-in-law and, of course, my grandchildren. I made many great friends there. In the spring of 2010, I met John, a retired army colonel who had been widowed for two years. We shared a love for dancing and traveling, and then hiking after discovering beautiful Sedona, Arizona, on one of our trips.

In March of 2013, John and I married and moved to Sedona. That summer, we planned a short road trip up north to hike through Zion National Park and then drive up to see Bryce Canyon. As our first stop, we spent the night in Tuba City, Arizona, and visited the Hopi Mesas. We had been trying to make contact with a Hopi guide, but to no avail. That is the only way you can go into the mesas to see the actual villages of the Hopi. So after checking in to the hotel, we drove out to see as much as we could on our own. Outside the Third Mesa, we stopped in a small gift shop. I wanted to purchase a kachina doll.

I have Indian heritage on my father's side and, living in Sedona, I feel a special kindred spirit with the Indian tribes who came here for their special ceremonies and events. Looking around at all the dolls displayed on the walls, I did not feel drawn to any of them and they were very expensive, so I began asking questions about the intriguing symbols on the dolls.

I was told that very few dolls are represented by female gender. They brought one out from the back that was made for a kachina maiden, a little girl. She had a star painted on her cheek, with something like a cloud and lightning bolts coming out of both sides of her head. I was suddenly dumbstruck remembering back to my childhood when I had experienced my first miracle.

It all flashed before me standing there holding that wooden doll. I was three years old and staying in my grandmother's home on her South Texas dairy farm. My mother was out in the back hanging laundry on the clotheslines when I came out from around the front of the house to the back to use the outhouse.

As I ran up the step to open the door to the wooden structure, my mother said, "Wait, Beatrice, until this truck goes by." She later told my grandmother she didn't know why she said it. There was a truck approaching on the county road where the property sat, but there was a thick row of trees between the backyard and the road concealing the outhouse. As I stood there in my little sundress with my hand on the door, an ear-splitting crash of thunder broke the silence. I have no memory of the actual lightning strike, but Mother said she heard me scream as she was thrown to the ground. She was about forty feet from me and said there was a huge column of fire where I had been standing.

Grandmother came running out of the house, she told me later, and carried me into the house, placed me on her bed, and called the doctor. There was nothing scorched or burned on me as I lay there unconscious, not even singed hair. The only evidence of a fire was a tiny burn on my cheek in the form of a five-pointed star.

I remember waking up and seeing a stack of large stone steps going from my head up to the sky so high up they grew smaller and smaller and disappeared. Living in Sedona, I have seen several "metaphysical" themed paintings with the familiar stone staircases leading up through the sky.

The doctor later pronounced me okay and left some salve for the burn. It seemed to be a mystery, they agreed, why a bolt of lightning would come out of a fair weather cloud on a nice laundry day. They speculated that had I been inside the structure, I would have been killed or badly burned by the metal exhaust pipe that went up through the roof.

The next day while taking a nap, I remember dreaming of leaving my little body and going up to the ceiling. I stayed up there and "flew" into the living room, where some adults were visiting and talking below me, but they couldn't see me. I continued along the ceiling and opened the back screen door and flew out above the house and around the yard, feeling such joy I had never known. Finally, I saw an ice-cream cone and flew over to it and the event (dream) ended. Thereafter at times in my life while totally awake with closed eyes, I would leave my body, flying to other lands and places—sometimes out into the universe of stars and nebulas—but that is another story.

Back at the Indian shop, I bought the kachina doll and she is now on the wall in my guest room where I pray and meditate. I told the young man behind the counter how we had hoped to connect with a Hopi guide and he picked up the phone and made a call to his father, who turned out to be the guide with whom we had left so many messages. A meeting was arranged and we would return the next morning to be driven through all the mesas, listening to the vivid history of the Hopi people and meeting several of them.

The kachina doll I purchased was unusually large and fragile and so the packing of it became a challenge. The owner of the shop appeared with packing material and set about protecting the doll for travel. As we shared our trip plans, he got out his special map and took my husband through the best routes, taking us around a major road closing so we could avoid many miles out of our way.

The morning we left, John pulled out from the hotel in the wrong direction. He finally found a turnaround and we were on our way. About forty miles down the road, we came to our intersection with the highway north. We waited for traffic to go by and then pulled out onto the highway. We passed a couple of vehicles and saw a white pickup ahead. Before we could close in behind the truck, we saw things falling out of the back. There was no tailgate and large logs of firewood were bouncing onto the road. John applied the brakes and we were able to avoid being hit by any of them. The truck pulled over and we drove on by, thankful for the delayed start that put us far behind that truck. Had we not made a little wrong turn as we left the hotel, we could have been right behind it when that wood started bouncing out on the road.

Later as we encountered the road we had been warned not to take, we were astounded to find there was no warning sign posted about the closing 20 miles ahead. We knew then we were blessed to have been given the alternate route. We had a wonderful trip through the parks and ended up at Lake Powell, where we had a reservation for one night. As we drove through the gate to the park, the attendant told us that had we been thirty minutes later, we would not have been allowed in due to the government shut downs of all national parks.

These are the kinds of things that can happen without our intentional participation, and we should appreciate them and express our gratitude every time they occur. In the lightning strike event, my mother listened to that still small voice and reacted in obedience, and my very life was affected.

Other seemingly coincidental events occur more often after we open ourselves through repetition in union with our divine natures. Synchronicity is a popular term for these seemingly coincidental events that can take our lives beyond our natural state and into the supernatural realm. Experiencing synchronicity in our lives is evidence that we are growing spiritually and aligning with our Creator and with one another. Thus, "freaky," unexplainable events where we interact with a situation or another person finally can be explained. Do not ever think these are just random thoughts or events, but take note and react with gratitude and appropriate action. In this way, you will propagate more and more miracles in your life. Synchronicity will become a common experience in your life.

Chapter 6

So You're Not Holy Enough?

We need to make our own miracles, it is a wasted exercise to just wait for miracles to happen; they need a spark of energy and desire to make them come true.
~ Steven Redhead, THE SOLUTION

After all the planning, all the money, all the dedicated world leaders, all the technical advances and increased head knowledge, where have we found ourselves in the world today? Have we fixed the problem of world hunger or even touched a solution for mass starvation occurring even now?

Blessed Mother Teresa did all she could and, thank God, millions were helped through her influence and dedication. But one lone lady in touch with her divine source of love cannot overwhelm the tide of a world of unawakened souls. Most of the time, we operate in the realm of our own mortality, putting ourselves first and foremost, wanting to get to the top, succeed at all costs, greedy for more "stuff" and power, millions of dysfunctional souls all seeking unconditional love and awash in misplaced ideas of how to secure it.

We have a disgraceful history of war after war, where millions of young men and women have been sacrificed out of nations, killed in their youth or horribly maimed—and to what purpose? Before long, another dictator or single-minded leader rises in fear of—or hatred for—another race or country and we commit the same insanity of war again.

I want you to know that just as we have used our power to create the world we have today, one with unsatisfying self-love, so we are beginning to connect with the Divine within to create one filled with love, joy, peace, and abundance for ourselves and all mankind.

I myself am a great study for a before-and-after life of contrast between an unawakened state of being and a connected, aligned awareness with our Creator God. With the hope of convincing you of your own cocreative power to produce miracles, I need to share that dark and unpleasant part of my life with you. There are choices and actions I took in an ignorant and suffering state of left brain logic and I am not proud of what transpired. It is important that you see the difference in choices I made during the second part of my life after I was awakened to who I really was.

My parents loved me and my siblings but, as in many cases, their generation was forced into living through tremendous hardships. My father's mother, my granny, had ancestors who walked the "Trail of Tears" from North Carolina to the Indian Reservations in Oklahoma. Thousands starved during that heartbreaking march. Try to imagine the deep resentment of Native Americans who, for thousands of years, roamed this beautiful land of abundance. That life was taken from them and their future generations because of the greed and deception of some of the early settlers. Then, years later, the Dust Bowl drought forced another migration out of the stricken Midwest. These conditions made it impossible for many families to create a loving and safe environment in their households. Most thoughts and efforts were turned toward survival.

Granny and Granddad had moved from Oklahoma to South Texas with their two daughters and two sons. Having no means of owning house or property, they hired out as sharecroppers. Fortunately, my daddy and his brother were healthy strapping boys and contributed to the financial stability of the family. The only memory I have of Granny was her lying ill in her bed in the living room, dipping snuff and yelling at me and my sister at every occasion it seemed. She was one angry woman and I emulated her in my early adult life, until I was set free from that source of hate and anger. Today, I can see how the treatment of her and her people had left her with a bitterness that bound up her heart. She had no love to give to anyone, not even herself.

The instability on my mother's side of the family started when my grandfather divorced my grandmother for a younger woman. I don't know and don't care about the story behind that. But grandmother had to raise two daughters on four hundred acres of farmland in South Texas. Enter my future daddy and his brother to help her on the farm.

As fate and normal hormones took over, these two young brothers fell in love with my mother and her sister. Two ill-suited marriages occurred and I and my siblings were brought into this world.

My grandfather's family were all educated and held what were considered professional positions: there were teachers, dentists, business owners, cattle ranchers, and a postmaster as I recall. I don't believe my mother ever forgave herself for marrying "beneath the family" until she was near her deathbed. She finally realized that what she considered as bad choices and regrets of what "could have been or was" did not matter. She came to know she was more than this mortal life and she embraced the unconditional love that filled her heart with peace at last. When that happened, I also received an influx of love she could then demonstrate to me and my siblings before she passed away.

My daddy was a fun-loving, talented, and hardworking man. He was a jack-of-all-trades and, at one time, became a very good home builder. Mother handled the financial matters while daddy brought home the paychecks. At one time, between jobs, he sang and played guitar with a rock group called Bill Haley and the Comets. I remember making a record in my grandmother's living room where Daddy was recording a song. He called me over and handed me the microphone and told me to sing something. I did not hesitate to sing my heart out with one of my favorites, "Jesus Love Me." I think my sister still has that old 78 record.

Daddy loved fishing and we went on many trips to Padre Island or in the many lakes and rivers across Texas. We moved almost every six months while Daddy looked for home construction work: framing, sheetrock hanging and finishing, painting.

He was very talented and meticulous and when builders saw his work, they put him on the large executive homes. The problem was Daddy had eventually become a weekend alcoholic and I guess he had a soft heart for the ladies because every Saturday night, Daddy returned home late at night with no money in his wallet.

On Fridays, our routine life started with cashing Daddy's paycheck and going for "supper," usually barbeque sandwiches or hamburgers. Then after a trip to supermarket to get a week's food, we would head to the drive-in movie. It was like clockwork. We saw every movie and kept up with every serial of *Tarzan*. But, oh, how my siblings and I dreaded Saturday nights. Without fail it seemed, Daddy would drive off early evening to have his beer. We never saw him drink the beer because Mother would not allow it in the house or even coffee for some reason so he also left early every morning. We kids also had to cope with prohibition in the house: No comic books allowed at a time when all kids collected them. We relished going to someone's house and reading the forbidden *Superman* or *Richie Rich* comics of that era.

Yes, Mother had strange ideas about the most common things and although we did not go to church, she somehow belonged to a sect that only had two congregations in Texas—one on the North

Texas border with Oklahoma, and the other in the Texas Valley close to Mexican border. Since we didn't live in those towns, we never went to church but there were summer conferences held in state parks once a year. Mother took us to those events whenever possible. That was when I learned a little about Jesus and was even baptized in a creek when I was twelve. I loved all the Bible stories about Jesus and I wanted to have my sins washed away. When I came up out of the water, I felt clean as snow, like I had never fibbed or disobeyed my parents.

We should be mindful of how receptive the thoughts and impressions of adolescents are when cultures or sects teach about either a vengeful God or one of unconditional Love. What a difference that alone could make in our world.

I eventually discovered that my mother believed that an unconfessed sin of any kind—from murder to drinking alcohol—would result in Jesus returning and throwing you into a fiery pit to be burned up instantly. This, she noted, was a more loving form of punishment than eternal torture as some erroneous religions taught. I suspect that as an impressionable little girl, I wondered if my own father could be pressed to do something like that with me if I disobeyed him.

Mother and Daddy were constantly fighting and running each other down. No wonder we kids didn't think much of ourselves; talk about inferiority complexes—we had them. On the rare occasion when we visited anyone in their home as a family, we were expected to sit politely.

"Children are to be seen and not heard," they reminded us.

Then there was the constant moving. Usually about six months after enrolling in a new school, we would come home to find Mom packing and soon, we piled into our old junky car or pickup and headed to another Texas town hoping Daddy could find work.

Being so talented, he always did, and our routines started over. I learned never to make a friend at school because they would want me to spend the night at their house (we called it a slumber party). Then I would be expected to have them stay over at my house. That is the way it was with girls. But after a few humiliating Saturday nights with Mother and Daddy fighting and cursing and sometimes neighbors calling the police, I knew it was better to just be a loner at school.

By the time I turned fifteen, I was begging Mother to divorce my father. Daddy had turned into a full-fledged alcoholic, and we were finding whiskey bottles all over the house hidden in various places. One time, he came home drunk at 2:00 a.m. and held us all at bay with a shotgun. Mother told me to phone Granddad who lived several miles away. My daddy looked hard at me and told me not to touch the phone. When he wasn't looking, I ran over and dialed the number, but he grabbed the phone and hung it up.

My granddad answered the phone only to hear a dial tone. Suspicious and worried, he drove over to our house, walked in, and confronted my father. Daddy started laughing and lowered the gun, informing us the gun wasn't loaded. My granddad walked over, took the gun, and decked Daddy, sending him careening across the room—just another crazy Saturday night in our family.

A few years later on my fifteenth birthday, without even my mother being aware, Daddy took me shopping and bought me a very expensive record player and some 45's. For the first time in my life, we were living in a nice house in a middle class neighborhood in Dallas. There had been two years of work in the suburbs and I was in my sophomore year at school.

Daddy was trying to make a good life for us and it was painful to see him break promises to attend school events, always apologizing for missing them or, even worse, showing up drunk.

Right after Daddy gave me that record player, he disappeared for six months. My grandfather paid our bills while Mother did some sewing and babysitting, never hearing a word from Daddy. I remember answering a knock on the door one Saturday morning and there he stood, looking like a bum. He had several days of beard and was dirty and smelly. He had been "riding the rails" he told me. My heart broke at the sight of him.

Mother came to the door and would not let him in. She had filed for divorce and we were already planning to move back to Grandmother's to help her with the dairy farm. I didn't see him again until I was nineteen and working in Illinois. That encounter turned out to be a disaster and I almost lost my job.

I had no desire to see him again after that until decades later after we had moved to our country home. I had written him a few times and received letters back from a woman who was living with him. It was she who called and told me he was in a bad way and I drove up to stay with him a few days. By then, I had only love and compassion in my heart for him. We talked about what was ahead for him. With fear in his eyes, he told me that his sins had caught up with him. After explaining what I knew about God's unconditional love for all, his fear disappeared and we both shared tears of gratitude.

Six months later, I received another call from the hospital to come quickly as he was dying. I drove for three hours praying to get there in time. I walked into his room alone and unprepared for the sight of that respirator jerking his head with every breath. His eyes were closed and his swollen face had a yellow pallor. I approached the bed and gently took his hand, searching for something to say.

To this day, I am puzzled by my final words to him but I suppose he just wanted me to be there when he passed to the other side. My parting words to him were, "You are a tough old bird, aren't you, Daddy?"

Immediately, the monitor started screaming and I saw the flat line of his heart beat. Nurses came running and ushered me out of the room. I returned a few days later with my family and took his ashes home with us. Later, I would join with my brother in spreading them on the waves of Padre Island, his favorite place to fish. I was able to feel his love and gratitude once again.

I recall all of this not to agonize over my childhood. As I stated earlier, I have no bitterness in my heart towards my parents. Sometimes Mother would stay up half the night sewing me a skirt I wanted to wear the next day to school. She kept a spotless house and cooked wonderful meals on a puny budget. I was a good little girl and was never even spanked by my parents, spanking being the norm for correcting children in those days. They did the best they could amid all the turmoil in their lives.

Thanks to my exposure to the character of Jesus in my early life, I held to an abhorrence of lying and an unwavering respect for telling the truth. My parents also instilled in me a strong work ethic, which has framed my life of achievement.

I used to think the most significant event in my life that has made me who I am today was my miraculous encounter with the spirit of Christ in 1974. Yes, it brought in a whole new way of life for me. But I now know that the event most responsible for the person I have become was being born into my dysfunctional, but loving family. All the heartbreak and adversity I was forced to overcome gave me a strength and determination that would not allow me to give up—ever—no matter the challenge I faced.

I hope you can approach any seemingly unfair or hopeless situations in your life from the same perspective. Use them to become strong so that you, too, can "rise to the occasion" when life comes at you with all its demands.

Chapter 7

Off To A Rocky Start

Nothing is predestined: The obstacles of your past can become the gateways that lead to new beginnings.
~ Ralph Blum

After Mother moved us from Dallas to the farm in South Texas, I embraced the stable lifestyle that a dairy requires. I loved the routine morning and afternoon milking, even on weekends, rising at four a.m. then gathering the cows from pasture for evening milking. It was a bit tougher after school started, but it was easy to make friends in that small community, and I was blossoming like a flower.

Summer vacations with my grandmother throughout my childhood had provided me with a role model I almost worshipped. Always full of laughter and praise and helping out any and everyone who needed it, my grandmother set a standard for life I could aspire to. Not only did she prosper running a dairy farm by herself, but she took in and cared for my aunt who was paralyzed with multiple sclerosis. As an adolescent during these summer visits, I was glad to help with this labor of love and amazed at the patience Grandmother displayed toward my aunt. Aunt Faye could take hours to get dressed for our weekly trip to town twenty miles away. I pushed her wheelchair around town as she shopped and stood by when she might take the better part of an hour to decide on a lipstick. Now as a teenager I had more patience and understanding with her.

Grandmother did not attend any church but we said grace at every meal. I loved to coax her into playing the grand piano in her living room. She knew hymns as well as ragtime. I have a memory of my paralyzed Aunt being baptized as an adult by a pastor. I also remember praying a lot for her to be able to walk, but she never got out of her wheelchair and after grandmother's death, Aunt Faye passed away in a nursing home, still loving Jesus.

As a teenager, I was thrilled to be back on the farm with Grandmother. Mom and I fixed up an old wooden "shot-gun" house Grandmother had moved on to the property. We updated it with sheetrock and paint and a nice linoleum floor. For the first time in our lives, we had real drapes on the windows. I had my own bedroom and painted it lavender and pink and invited my girlfriends over to spend the night.

I was having the time of my life as I found myself elected cheerleader and started dating the star running-back. I excelled in my studies and, for the first time, I made the honor roll and was elected class president my senior year, graduating as salutatorian.

My boyfriend was a grade below me; we became engaged before I left to enroll at the Bible College. One of my mother's relatives had offered to pay all my college costs so off I went on my first train ride all the way to Chicago.

After the first semester bills piled up and no financial aid from relatives arrived, I quit and rented a room from an elderly couple and took a waitress job in a family restaurant. I saved all my money and paid off the college debts. I walked home one day from work to find an ambulance taking the old man out of the garage. He had killed himself. I didn't blame him after the way his wife continually yelled and criticized him.

Next day, I bought a train ticket home to Texas and soon, my high school sweetheart and I enrolled at the nearby A & I University. With the birth of our first son, we both dropped out of school and by the time the third son was born six years later, our marriage was in trouble. My husband was a good man and had a good job with a bright future, but I was unhappy. In retrospect, I can see that I felt stifled and unchallenged, although I loved raising the children. With a lack of wisdom and maturity, I decided to get a divorce.

I found a job as office manager. I paid for my divorce, taking the furniture and giving him the car and TV. I rented a nice house a few blocks from my mother and stepdad near Padre Island. The boys and I spent every nice weekend on the island in my gently used station wagon, sleeping in the back and cooking hot dogs on the beach. We were happy and, in my innocence, I looked forward to a carefree life of joy.

Then I met a man. I honestly cannot remember where or how, but this nice Italian man invited me out to dinner. I suppose we had drinks because when he brought me home, I was totally inebriated. When he started kissing me and pushing me down on the sofa, I could not hold him back. He paid no attention to my crying "No," and I did not have the presence of mind to scream or kick. He tore through my panty hose and was on top of me, raping me in my drunken state. I don't remember him leaving. It was the late sixties and I was to learn that men did not believe that, "No means no!" I was also to learn that I sometimes attracted men who wanted to control or abuse me.

I then met a sailor who I was so attracted to I couldn't stay away from him. I had never experienced this kind of chemical attraction, but I soon realized he was an insanely jealous man. One night after a game of pool at a neighborhood bar, he pushed me up against a plate glass window. He accused me of flirting with another man with whom I had only politely responded to an inquiry. With glowering eyes and gnashing teeth, this man I adored threatened to push my head through the glass. He finally came to his senses and took me home, where I gratefully closed the door on him for the last time.

The terror was not over, however, as the next night after repeatedly ringing the doorbell and yelling at me, he attempted to come through my living room window. My fourteen-year-old brother was with me watching as this guy tore off the screen, put one leg inside, and started choking poor Phil with both hands. I had the ironing board up in the living room and took the hot iron and placed it almost to his face and he backed away. I called the police and never saw him again. My stepfather learned he had been transferred out to another base. Thank God!

Sometime later, my boss introduced me to an associate of his who had purchased a shipyard and was driving down from Houston every week. He was a divorced father of three girls and a perfect gentleman and, suddenly, I was riding around in a Cadillac, learning to drink gin and tonics and eat steak and lobster. Here was a mature gentleman who respected me and treated me like a lady. He seemed to love watching me experience life's adventures: my first deep-sea fishing excursion sitting in the fighting chair reeling in a kingfish; fine dining enjoying my first lobster tail. Trips to Padre Island now were spent in lawn chairs under a shady canopy with steaks on the grill and fishing poles in the surf. The boys and I were in heaven.

My trouble with men was not over, though. One night after a tiring day at work, I put my boys to sleep early, showered, and went to bed, leaving the bathroom door ajar as usual as a nightlight. I kept the windows open at night to allow the cool breeze from the bay to cool the house.

Sometime later, I was awakened to find it totally dark and someone on the bed on top of me. Still half asleep, I remember slurring out "Hey, what are you doing? Who are you?"

The guy actually gave me some name and then I was fully awake and realized what was going on. As far as I remember, the guy was fully clothed but I had only my panties on and lying on top of the towel. The guy was trying to pull down my panties and I quickly grabbed them with both hands. A struggle ensued and I found myself upside down hanging off the side of the bed, still clinging to my underwear for dear life. Then the guy landed his fist to my jaw and finally I had the presence of mind to let out a scream.

Suddenly he was off me and disappeared into the darkness of the hall. I made my way down the hall to the front door and locked it. I turned on the lights and searched the boys' rooms. Thankfully they were asleep and then, shaking with fear, I phoned the police. While waiting and talking with the dispatcher for about ten minutes, I noticed a wallet on the bed and she told me to open it and look for I.D. I pulled everything out—driver's license, all kinds of credit cards, etc. The dispatcher and I were still talking and wondering why the police were taking so long when this guy suddenly appeared in my doorway. He had something tied around his face under his eyes. I screamed as he ran straight toward me. My only thought was he had come back to kill me.

Over my screams, I now heard an approaching police siren and watched this guy scoop up as much of the cards on the bed as he could grab. Then I watched in amazement as he threw himself out my bedroom window. I had been sitting there going through his wallet for twenty minutes unaware that the screen was gone. That was how he had first entered the house.

Later, the police discovered the screen off in the boy's room and that was how he had returned. Now as I watched out the window still screaming, I saw him running through the yard with a flashlight beam following along. Another policeman stuck his head in the window, shined his light in my face and said, "Shut up, Lady!" The man got away that night.

My mother came over. Thankfully, the boys had slept through the whole thing, but I had to go downtown and have a photo taken of my black and blue cheek. The police took his license and other I.D. he had missed and, two days later, I was called in to the station and identified him in a lineup.

He worked down the street from my office and supposedly had followed me home from there. The police arrested him but tried to talk me out of pressing charges. He had a record of peeping-tom charges and they told me it would be a messy trial for a divorced good-looking woman like me. I felt a moral obligation to press charges and then they left me in a room alone with him. He pleaded with me to drop charges. He had a family. I persisted against them all and made the formal charge of "breaking and entering" and "attempted rape." Immediately he was out on bail. I worried about him returning to take revenge and suffered several sleepless nights. And then fate stepped in.

I returned home from work after picking up my boys from daycare to find a moving van parked in front and men carrying out all my furniture. Mother and my boys were standing in the yard watching this spectacle. My ex-husband and I may have been confused about who was making those payments. Contracts were always made in the husband's name in those days and it was too late to object to whatever misunderstanding there was. I watched in disbelief as two men walked by with dollies holding my refrigerator and stove. Mother took the kids home with her and I took off to buy a large ice chest in which to keep the milk and other items now piled up on the kitchen counter.

Next day, I rented an apartment near work and moved the kids and me into a cute little Section 8 apartment complete with fully equipped kitchen. We made pallets in the bedrooms and I sat in my only piece of furniture, a high back cane seat chair. My eldest son all of six years old would pull that chair up to the sink and wash dishes for me after supper every night and we felt safe and happy.

I continued to see Robert on most weekends. I declined his generous offer to buy me some furniture and soon, I had saved enough to get three bunk beds for the boys and a mattress for me. I then purchased a sofa, chair, and coffee table. Everything had to be new because when my oldest son had asked me where the furniture was going, I said boldly, "Boys, I got tired of that old furniture and told the movers to come haul it off. We're going to get some new stuff."

Robert and I were having marathon phone conversations every night and our love blossomed. I couldn't have been happier. A year later we were married and living in Houston.

Chapter 8
You Can't Buy Happiness

"To me every hour of the light and dark is a miracle,
Every cubic inch of space is a miracle."
~ Walt Whitman

I was now a privileged woman of leisure but fate was not done with me and I was about to go through the worst time in my life. Entering Robert's world of dinner parties and conventions required my moving up in wardrobe from Penney's and Sears to Sakowitz and Neiman's. Soon, I had two furs, cocktail dresses, and all the accessories.

We designed and built a large home on eight acres complete with some cows, a horse, and a stocked pond. My boys were taking tennis lessons and having friends over to swim in our huge backyard pool. I had a girlfriend for the first time in my life and we played golf at a little nine-hole course nearby several times a week during school hours. I had everything a girl could dream of.

Problem was I was drinking scotch like it was plain water and so depressed I was going from one pill to the next in-between counseling. I quit one counselor after he told me I had so much anger in me that he feared I might kill my husband. I told him he was the one who needed therapy. But none of that helped and I despaired of the dark moods and lack of joy in the midst of all that *beautiful* life.

My husband was getting tired of seeing me sleep all day and stay up reading novels all night. We both liked to entertain and I was a good cook so our parties were well attended. We partied almost every night with our neighbors—eating, drinking, playing pool in the game room, mixing every cocktail known to man at our twelve-foot bar in the den.

I remember a night after one of these gatherings. I was really drunk and Robert was not exactly sober. We were in our huge shower together and I was yelling at him and then I started pounding on his chest. He slapped me across the face. That shame-filled event jarred me into realizing how pitiful my life had become. What was wrong with me?

I saw no way out of this deep sadness that enveloped me everywhere I turned. In addition, I began to suffer from migraine headaches that kept me in bed for two or three days at a time with mind-numbing pain.

One day, I was particularly desperate for relief from the darkness in my soul. As if watching a movie, I saw myself open the bottle of pain pills and swallow a handful, thinking I could just sleep and never wake up to have to face my despondency again. When Robert came home and couldn't wake me, he drove me to the hospital and they pumped my stomach. We returned home both in despair over what to do with me.

That event was the beginning for my awakening to the hell I was creating for myself. I had read a book called *Chariots of the Gods* by an author making the case that God was an astronaut from outer space who came and seeded our planet. My few experiences with God from my youth were a distant memory but enough for me to hope a loving God might truly exist.

I arose late in the morning a few weeks after my attempted suicide. The boys and hubby were gone for the day. I woke up, lit a cigarette, and stumbled to the bathroom mirror. There I stood with smoke swirling around my head, stinging my eyes still ringed with makeup from the night before. Tears began to trickle down my face and I heard myself crying out, "God, if you are real, please help me. I'm ruining everyone's life and I can't seem to stop. Please, please, help me," I sobbed. Those empty eyes stared back at me in the silence. Finally, I wiped my face and declared to the mirror, "Nobody is going to help you."

That night, as usual, I couldn't get to sleep. I got up from bed about midnight and went to the den looking through the bookcase for a mystery novel, one I hadn't already read. I belonged to a book club but sometimes I could read through a book in two nights. As I peered up to the top shelf, my eyes fell on a Bible I had kept with me from my childhood.

I sat down with my cigarettes and lighter and opened the book. Since it was the beginning of the New Testament, I started reading right there in the book of Matthew. Very soon, I was completely absorbed in the stories of Jesus' life and times. I discovered that Mark and Luke's writings were the same stories, but told from their perspective of the things Jesus did. Then I began reading the book of John. I would soon learn that John was known as the beloved disciple. He recorded the words of Jesus that were all about the love of God, the Father of all.

I became convinced that Jesus had been a real man who was born on this Earth and knew where he came from, the Source of All, the creator God. He not only knew he was a Son but he said we were all sons of the same Creator.

The words I was reading seemed to have a life of their own. They were tangible and I took them into my heart as truth, a thing I held in high regard. I was accepting the truth that I was the progeny of the Creator of the Universe and a recipient of pure unconditional love. There was nothing I had done or could do that would stop that flow of Divine love for me. This was the way I felt about my own children, and my heart swelled up with a sense of gratitude I had never experienced in my life. I couldn't speak. I couldn't form any thought in my head except gratitude for love.

I am loved just the way I am—even in spite of the way I am, kept ringing through my head. Waves of gratitude rolled over me. I dropped to my knees and started thanking Jesus and God and the men who had followed him and recorded these words. I had an overwhelming desire to give them something in return and so I found myself giving my heart, myself, my life, my treasures—everything to this tangible force of love.

All of a sudden, I felt a presence, an invisible force of some kind leaving my body and it actually made a swooshing sound as it left. In my mind's eye, I saw a dark vapor dissipate up through the ceiling. Then immediately in came a tidal wave of joy that coursed through my veins and seemed to saturate my entire body. Tears were streaming down my face and I was blubbering thank-yous and oh-my-Gods.

Sometime later, I found myself back in the Bible reading through the book of Acts that began when the followers of Jesus gathered in the upper room of a house after his ascension from this Earth. I read the description by the disciple Luke, who, I would learn later, was a doctor and included many details in his recording of events from long ago.

There were 120 people praying and waiting as they had been instructed by Jesus before he left the Earth.[7] "Wait and pray for power from on high," he had said.

They had been there several days, eating and praying together when suddenly, an invisible force fell on and in them. Their reaction was similar to what I had just experienced as they began to worship and praise God. I continued to read the description of them speaking in different languages to others present in the city. Now, I recalled that experience as a student in the Bible College upon hearing that salvation was a gift from God and how

---

[7] Luke 24:59

I had begun praying in a foreign language to express my gratitude.

So it was that I now understood I had received an infilling of what the Bible called the Holy Spirit, which is also known as Life Force or Chi, as well as the feminine aspect of God.[8] All these years later, I have come to understand that experience as connecting to the Source of All. When you experience that union, it is with joy and gratitude at being empowered to overcome addictions and other obstacles to your own happiness. What a glorious gift it was to me. Perhaps this is the experience labeled as being "born again" by many evangelists.

My closest friends saw the change in me and told me I was just a new *convert* and would calm down after a while. I noticed three days later that I was no longer smoking and it was as if I had never smoked. It was the same with the depression. I had so much love and joy in me there was no room for that darkness. I only felt love for everyone. It turned out I would never need another anti-depressant. There was no more cussing or drinking for me at the parties. I just didn't even like the taste anymore. I did still enjoy a glass of wine or champagne now and then. In later years, I was able

---

[8] Holy Spirit the Feminine Aspect of the Godhead, C 1993 JJ Hurtak Phd.

to socially drink at times if I wished with no fear of addition. This was true freedom and deliverance.

Immediately, my education in religions and the ways of God began at the nearby Christian bookstore where I was led to books by deceased authors like Andrew Murray, Watchman Nee, and others from the era known as the Great Outpouring of Spirit around the world. I was using a huge Strong's Concordance to study the Bible. I challenged those teachings about hell and heaven such as the "rapture" theory, which later prompted the series, *Left Behind*.

To this day, I don't know why I was so blessed to receive such a life-changing epiphany. We all have our own path to enlightenment and surrender. Most people do not have to experience the depths of despair as I did before reuniting with their Creator God. If you find yourself on a destructive path, it is my hope you will invite God (by whatever name) into your situation as soon as you find yourself in difficulty. Know with all your heart that you can reconnect with your Creator within just as I did. Christian, Muslim, Jewish— whatever—just embrace the God of Unconditional Love. Your own life of miracles will follow.

Chapter 9

Expect and Demand Guidance

"Intuition will tell the thinking mind where to look next."
~ Jonas Salk (1914-1995)

M y joy-filled days were spent pouring through the Bible and other books. I was seeking to know the truth about who God was. I knew of no one who shared my passion for this intensive search. My Christian and Jewish friends had no interest in any Bible study of their own.

Then, one day, the doorbell rang and I found two ladies holding a little Bible and some magazines. They wanted to come in and study the Bible with me. I literally pulled them into the house. I told them all about how Jesus had appeared to me and changed my life. They seemed especially impressed that I no longer smoked. These two religious ladies came twice a week for several months and I finally was persuaded to attend their worship hall nearby, dragging my three boys along.

My husband was incensed. He had no regard for this religious sect and was very upset over my involvement. Soon, my car was full of magazines that I purchased but never intended to deliver. I just wanted to please my two Bible study friends. My sons hated the boring meetings where converts took turns practicing their door-to-door presentations. I did not feel I belonged there but I knew I didn't belong in churches preaching hellfire and damnation.

I began to question these ladies on several points in their literature but they did not have any answers. They would write down my challenges and questions about their faith and they would bring back the answers at our next meeting. They never tried to dampen my devotion to Jesus Christ but they didn't mention him much either. Still, I was happy I had finally found a group I could study with and share what I was learning about God.

My two ladies were elated when I finally told them I was going to be baptized and join the fellowship. That evening, I told my husband of my plans. I was totally unprepared for his reaction to this news.

With his mouth set hard, he looked me in the eye and said, "If you do that, I will divorce you."

I could feel the anger seething inside him and I knew he meant it. I now had a huge decision to make. I loved and trusted God for saving my life from that unbearable existence with depression. In gratitude, I had given it back to him. If his plan was for me to join this organization and tell others about unconditional love, well then, how could I now go back on my word?

I had to know I was hearing from God. If I was being called to give up this wonderful life for me and my sons and turn my back on a good man who loved me, then I would do so. I did not have the maturity then to know that God would never want anything for me or my husband that did not result in joy, peace, love, and abundance.

I prayed and pondered through most of the night about what to do. I pleaded with God to let me know clearly what He wanted me to do. Earlier that day, my Doberman puppy had run into our barbed wire fencing in the pasture and I had taken her to the vet for stitches. He was known as the best vet in South Texas and had wrapped her leg up in tight bandages. I placed her in the crate to keep her still for the night.

The next morning after my night of prayer, I went to check on Angel and found she had torn through her bandage and was licking her wounds. I called the vet to tell them I was bringing her back in. That vet could not see her but his partner would be able to take care of her. As I sat in the waiting room, I was reading one of the church's books.

The vet was walking by and stopped to ask me what I was reading. I told him it was a book about the kingdom of God and asked him if he knew anything about that particular sect. He said "No, but I will be meeting at my home tonight with a bunch of people who love God. You are welcome to come join us. We just sing and share together." He gave me his address and directions to his house.

Soon, I was taking Angel back home. When Robert came home from work, I told him about the invitation and asked him if he would go with me. I was relieved and very surprised to hear him say, "Yes." He had never shown much interest in my Bible studies and seemed a little skeptical about my zealous love for God. Being an Aggie, I think he was impressed and reassured that the veterinarian was hosting the gathering, but whatever the reason, I felt a ray of hope that my marriage could be saved.

That evening, we felt a little awkward walking into a group of people sitting around on the floor in a circle chatting. We introduced ourselves and joined them on the floor as one guy strummed his guitar. The group proceeded to sing songs we had never heard. Some of them would occasionally raise their arms up with closed eyes. I realized these people were feeling the way I did about God and they had a connection going.

I thought to myself, *I wish they would sing something I know so I could join in the worship with them*. Immediately, the guitar player stopped what he had started to play and started the Lord's Prayer in song. Of course I knew the words and my heart leaped for joy and with tears escaping my tightly closed eyes, I raised my hands in worship and song. Later, I would replay that scene as I read in the Bible[9] *"Speaking to yourselves in psalms and hymns and spiritual songs, singing and making melody in your heart to the Lord...."*

At the end of the song, it grew very quiet. That sweet silence was then broken when the guitar player stated authoritatively: "Take my hand, I am walking beside you."

Then silence again. After a few moments, everyone opened their eyes and stirred around. We chatted a bit and soon everyone was listening as I shared about my recent Spiritual encounter and how it had changed my life. I also shared how I had prayed during the night for guidance and direction on my newfound journey with God.

---

[9] Ephesians 5:19

The vet then asked if I knew who had spoken to me about "taking his hand" earlier and I replied, "I think it was Jesus or the Holy Spirit."

He then asked me if I would like them to pray with me and I said I would. They gathered around and some placed their hands on my head and shoulders.

The next day, I was ready to share my exciting experience with my study sisters at our scheduled afternoon meeting but they never showed up. Two days later, the same thing happened, a no-show for our meeting.

I never saw or heard from them again. They had all been excited about my scheduled baptism and membership and yet there never was a call to see what happened to me.

I had my answer from God and a new respect for my husband who clearly responded to my misdirected path in a way to steer me back onto my personal path. My question to the vet and his response led to the resulting miracle of that encounter with what I later learned was a charismatic home group. What if the vet had not questioned me about that book? What if I had not inquired about the religious group? We must be open and expectant as we seek guidance or we can miss subtle directions. God doesn't just push our bodies along and speak through us like a ventriloquist. When united in purpose and desire with the Divine, we become sensitive to that "still small voice" and become facilitators of miracles around us and others who cross our path. Aligned with God, we become aligned with others as mentioned earlier in explaining synchronicity. Apparently, even my dog, another of God's creatures, was aligned to play a role in a miraculous event that would have a profound impact upon my life and others.

I do not want to cast aspersions upon the group of people in that sect with whom I studied. We are all on our personal journeys and times of enlightenment as to God's nature and our own life purpose.

I would learn later that my sister living in Oklahoma had joined that same sect of organized religion a few months prior to my having that first home visit. In her experience she has known it as a blessing in her life.

You need not be a lone journeyman in this world. Ask and expect help when you go within to connect with the One who is all wisdom, strength, love, and peace. Had my husband not forcefully questioned my decision, I would not have asked for guidance from what I now consider my go-to guy. All these years later, I now feel connections with other departed souls like the prophet Daniel who, like me, was curious about the end of the age within which we all live. In 1980, my curiosity drove me to research the development of religions since the death of Christ in AD 30 up to the present time. At the time of that study, I read the book of Daniel being completely oblivious to the similarities between this Old Testament prophet and myself. We had even both fasted for three weeks on water only as we sought understanding about the matter. It was only recently I remembered the manuscript I had mailed to myself. I unsealed it and read through it again, astounded at the prophetic events I interpreted at the time and so described. I will be polishing up that manuscript and posting it on my web site.

A final word of instruction from this chapter: Whether you are on the receiving end or the facilitating end of a miracle, it is critical that you be in a state of awareness and anticipation. Then you must follow that still small voice of direction.

Chapter 10

The Dark Side

You will face your greatest opposition when you are closest to your biggest miracle.

~ Shannon L. Alder

Not too long after this major crisis was averted, I began to suffer a recurring nightmare. I would have the same dream and wake up with a feeling of terror coursing through my body. Our bedroom opened out through sliding glass doors onto a deck overlooking the pool. The dream always began with a black wolf with glowing red eyes walking right through those doors, approaching my bed. As he neared the bed, I would wake up, feeling this intense cold chill come over my body, afraid to look down and find that creature beside me. As stark fear subsided, I would lie there trying to stay awake because sleep only brought back the dream.

By this time, I had already read through the entire Bible and was studying in the New Testament daily, along with books I would be steered to. I knew I was being taught by Spirit because inevitably, the book I purchased would turn out to be about the subject I was reading in the Bible. This was no surprise to me, as I took these recorded words of Jesus to heart: "But the Helper, the Holy Spirit, whom the Father will send in my name, will teach you all things and bring to your remembrance all that I said to you.[10]

I began to relate my nightmare to the incidents when Jesus would cast demons and illness out of people he encountered. I had been delivered from so much already and now I wanted to be free of the dark force invading my sleep.

One morning after a night of terror from these dreams, I pleaded in prayer for help. I then randomly opened up my Bible and there in the book of Psalms at the top of the page I saw: "A Prayer for Deliverance." I had my answer. So now what? I had no church or pastor but I was learning to trust in that Guiding Hand that was holding mine.

A few days later, I was reading the Houston newspaper and saw a notice for a ladies' luncheon

---

[10] John 14:26

to be held in a church fellowship hall. Still hoping to find someone else who could relate to my passion for this spiritual journey I was on, I decided to drive into town. I chatted with the ladies at my table and then the speaker took the podium and gave an interesting talk. He was pastor of the largest Baptist church in Houston.

As the meeting ended, I turned to the lady on my left and said, "Do you know anything about the deliverance ministry?"

She stared at me a moment and then said quickly, "Lets go outside and talk about that."

It turned out she and her husband were in a deliverance ministry sanctioned by the top leadership in the Baptist Church.

As we became acquainted, I related my epiphany story and how my life was so dramatically changed after my encounter with the Spirit of Christ in my home. I then explained about my dreams and how I had been directed to seek out deliverance. This lady I shall call Sara told me I must first get a "covering" from my husband. I would have to make sure he was in agreement with me coming to receive prayer for deliverance.

That evening, I told Robert what had transpired with the dream, the Psalm, and the meeting in town. Then I told him I wanted his permission to go meet with this couple for prayer or whatever

Beatrice Schuller

their ministry consisted of. He said it was fine but that he did not want to go with me. My response: "I don't blame you and I'm not looking forward to it myself." In fact, I was nervous as hell and was I not convinced of the obvious divinely driven directive, I would not have agreed to the ordeal.

At the first meeting, I repeated a description of my spiritual encounter and subsequent events, including the charismatic home meeting. They asked me if I "spoke in tongues." I explained about my occasional singing in a strange Jewish-sounding dialogue during my "quiet time" of prayer and reflection. At that moment, a distant memory returned to me of speaking in that same language once while attending the Bible College after high school. I suppose I had filed it far away as something unsuitable for discussion, but here it was in the forefront of my mind again. I proceeded to tell the couple how it had happened.

As a freshman I was enjoying the camaraderie of dorm life and our nightly prayer circle when I had my first "experience with Jesus." As we sat on the floor taking turns praying, I had a vision of Christ floating above and in the middle of our circle. My eyes were closed but I could see him in his white robe in my mind's eye. I did not tell the girls about it for fear they would think I was making it up. Sometime later in a class taught by one of the graduates still in training, a scripture he quoted caught my attention and I later visited him in his office to discuss it. I remember the idea of the passage was that salvation was a free gift and could not be earned.[11] The conundrum I questioned with him was the doctrine of conditional salvation being taught in the classes. The two concepts were not compatible as I explained to him. As I reviewed the scripture, it seemed to penetrate my very soul. Suddenly, I was seized by an emotion of tremendous love and gratitude and jumped up from my chair, ran out the door and down the hall. I opened the door to our little chapel and ran into one of the rows of pews and fell on my knees with uplifted face. Instead of a prayer in English, out came this Jewish-sounding prayer accompanying my joy-filled tears.

Later, I was so excited about this strange event I began sharing it with anyone on campus who would stand still long enough for me to tell it. We were scheduled to travel to a nearby church and, as part of our credits, were required to give a "testimony" of our own choosing. I let it be known that I was going to tell of my marvelous experience and how eternal life was a free gift offered to all who would accept it.

We lined up to board the bus, but I was taken aside by one of the instructors and told I was not to

---

[11] Eph. 2:8

give testimony of my "speaking in tongues" to anyone. When I protested, he explained that I had just been overcome by emotion and that speaking in tongues was not "for today." I was crushed in my spirit and confused that such a wonderful feeling was not allowed in church. Later, my roommate would explain about the "holy roller" church and the so called "awful antics" that went on there. I never mentioned the incident again.

I finished the detailed explanation of my youthful experience to the ministry couple sitting patiently before me. I sensed a challenging tone in the husband's response. Would I submit to a testing of my tongues, he asked. I had no idea what they meant by "testing," but felt that guiding hand holding me tight and told them, "Sure." Another meeting was scheduled for that test. I left wondering what kind of adventure I had begun with these people.

I was surprised to find the pastor waiting when I arrived the next week. He told me he wanted me to speak in my tongues and he would ask a few questions. I explained that I only experienced it after I kind of ran out of ways to express my love for God or Jesus and then I used the other language. He said for me to proceed and I began with my little recitation of love talk to God and then slipped into the so-called "tongues."

The pastor then said, "I am addressing the spirit who is now speaking through Beatrice." He asked me several questions and I answered them for him—in English, of course. I only remember the last question and answer. It was "To the Spirit speaking in tongues, do you call Jesus Christ as Lord?" My answer was "Yes." I guess he considered it a rare miracle, because he then said, "This is one of the very few times I have found the Spirit of God speaking through a person." To me, the entire exercise was "much ado about nothing."

Years later after being awakened to the beautiful reality of the Divine Presence in every creature, I wondered at how limited a view we hold of ourselves most of our lives. The Spirit of God can speak through us as us in every language known to man, including our own if we choose to cooperate.

After I was accepted as a candidate for deliverance, I returned for several sessions with that couple. My life was placed on a fast track as I released deep-seated memories of shame and origins of stress, fears, and debilitating beliefs about myself. I continued to move into the gifts of the Spirit, along with my private studies of the metaphysical world now opened up to me.

Obviously, everyone does not need to be delivered in such a dramatic fashion as I just described. I do recommend that everyone spend time alone or with professional help to release emotional scars from the past, especially if suffered in early childhood. These can sabotage our lives as we mature and face new challenges.

I benefited greatly a few years ago from an audio set of the *Silva Life* series. By relaxing into a deeply meditative state, I released many blockages and false beliefs that had kept me from God's purpose for me. That is to live in peace, love, joy, and abundance.

I have been freed from the inferiority complex I carried from my childhood. I was astounded to learn at such a late state in my life how to appropriately express anger. Before my spiritual encounter, I would yell and throw things in a fit of anger. After that beautiful infilling of God's love, I would just be nonresponsive if someone hurt me physically or verbally. Sadly, hurt and resentment were just pushed down into my soul, later to manifest as heart attacks.

Neither of these actions is a healthy emotional response. Now I confront the ones doing the hurting with a calm delivery and ask them to treat me in a respectful way if they wish to have my company. To me, that is a welcome miracle in my new walk with God.

Chapter 11

Opened Doors

"Follow your instincts. That's where true wisdom manifests itself."

~ Oprah Winfrey

After a few sessions of "deliverance," my journey took another turn. This was our move to Kingwood, of which I recounted in Chapter 2 the healing in my home prayer meeting. That guiding hand was teaching me more about those miracles Jesus said we could all do and even greater. The healing of little Kevin built my faith and readied me for the lone journey ahead. I had no idea it would be just me and God against a multitude of challenges.

It was after we again moved to the country and built our home on twenty-five beautiful acres that I realized there would be no more church for me. One pastor of an Assembly of God church told me I had to leave his fellowship because I shared my revelation that the Spirit of Christ (annointing) actually resides in all mankind as a spark, awaiting a connection with the Divine.

Another pastor, a Baptist, told me he could not come to my home Bible study if I was teaching that there was no hell for sinners. I chuckled and told him, "Heaven forbid your ears should hear such devastating news."

And so I sustained my spiritual walk on our property, among the hardwoods and pine and the abundant wildlife. I began a very close walk with God as conditions around us took a turn for the worse.

The economy in Texas was in a downturn but we were grateful to have the cash to finish building our home, although we did a lot of the interior labor ourselves. I had taken some writing and computer courses at a nearby community college. My husband found some work selling machine tool parts, but he was a marine engineer, not a salesman, and we were barely surviving. Some of our friends filed for bankruptsy, but we had our home paid for and were basically debt free. All the children were on their own now, struggling to stay in college. We helped as much as we could and one joined the army.

New Year's Eve was coming around and I always took time at midnight to find a place to be alone and talk with God about the coming year. That night I bundled up, walked out back under the clear sky gazing up at a sea of stars and said something like, "Father, I don't know what to do with the rest of my life now that the children are gone. I give it to you first, carte blanche, to do with what you will. I will walk through any door you open. I love you and trust you and look forward to whatever we will be doing together. "

The very next day, I was perusing through our local county newspaper in the classifieds when a simple ad caught my attention: WRITER WANTED. There was only a phone number so later on I called it. To my surprise, I found myself speaking to the publisher of an advertising newspaper, the kind you find folded in a little rack inside businesses. I had seen this around our little town. They were looking for a reporter. I explained to the lady that I was not a journalist but she insisted I come in and talk with her. Later, I found her office in a little strip center and, before I knew it, I was on my way to a nearby town to report on a Chamber of Commerce meeting.

After taking notes and speaking with those who conducted the meeting, I headed back to the office, stopping to buy a *Houston Post*. Studying over the articles, I then wrote up my report and presented it to the owner. I was hired and even the meager salary did not dampen my enthusiasm. I did, however, feel a little like an imposter. I mean how could I call myself a journalist or a reporter when I had no credentials or experience? I was soon to discover that those things are not necessarily required when you are holding the hand of the Source of All That Is.

Two days later, I got a glimpse of what lay in store for me on this new venture, led and inspired by my Divine companion. Pat, the owner, strolled into my little cubicle with her squinted eyes and pimpled face, framed by oily uncombed hair. With a cigarette hanging from her lips, she began to outline the day's schedule. I grabbed my pad to take notes. "Congressman Barton will be here this afternoon for an interview. He's on his annual whistle stop tour through the district."

I was excited. I had never met my U. S. Representative, although I had voted for him. "Pat," I said, "can I sit in on the interview with you?" She ignored me and continued with her list of things for me to do. She turned to leave, looking over her shoulder she added, "Oh, by the way, you are doing the interview: three o'clock here in my office."

I was to learn a year later that Joe Barton, after that interview, had confided to one of his colleagues that he felt like he had been at the *Washington Post* that day I interviewed him. I served on his steering committee for two years and considered him a friend.

From the beginning, I edited my own copy. Pat could not spell and had no talent for designing ads either, so I took over that department—with no raise in salary. I could not bear to see the awful photos that occasionally appeared in the paper. Since we had our own darkroom at home, I added photography to my unpaid duties. Soon we were looking like a real newspaper and I was asked to join the Chamber of Commerce and chaired a committee to beautify our little town. With no raise in salary in sight, I told Pat that if she would not allow me to sell advertising on commission, I would have to look for work elsewhere.

Soon I was filling the paper with ads and working day and night. One day, I received a call from a triweekly full-page newspaper wanting me to come in and talk with them. They were offering me a job as editor and a nice salary. I was astounded and knew I could not handle such a position. It was a large enterprise with their own presses and sales staff, editorial and sports writers, composition department. I would be in charge of all that under this publisher sitting there in front of me. I told him I was neither qualified nor had the experience for this job.

He persisted with the offer, finally telling me, "I think the Lord led us to you to save our paper. We are in the red and need to make major changes to survive. You are key to those changes. We have seen the transformation you have made to that weekly paper you are working for."

A feeling of panic began to flow through me as I realized this offer was a challenge to my resolve to walk through any door that was opened as a spiritual calling. The most I could commit to was a three-week trial to see if I was up to the job. The publisher accepted my terms and I left to go and give two weeks' notice to Pat. Apparently, I was losing that job anyway. She told me she had already planned to close the paper and move to another county and publish an ad-only paper and so I went home to ponder the new opportunity before me.

I was given two days of preparation to work with the current editor and I watched with growing panic as she put a twenty-page newspaper together on a computer screen, drawing articles and ads from all departments. She added headlines and cut and pasted from one page and continued on another. It was an amazing feat. I would have only one more opportunity to watch, take notes, and ask questions. My first paper would be a special edition of an estimated thirty-six pages that would cover the county fair and rodeo edition.

The first day of my trial run as editor arrived for me at 4:00 a.m. I spent some time losing my coffee and fighting dry heaves before driving the eight miles into town. On the drive, I had a serious conversation about expecting help with the paper if this was an assignment I was to take on. If not, I would do the best I could and if not up to the task, I would simply tell them we all made a mistake and walk out the door. Upon arriving, I had to endure furtive glances from the employees and I could read their expressions like "Have the owners lost their minds?" and "This is going to be fun to watch."

I sat down at the monitor and it was like in the old cartoons, when a lightbulb appears on top of someone's head representing an idea. Yes, it was like putting a giant jigsaw puzzle together and, by midafternoon, it was ready to go to press.

Any editor will tell you that was definitely a miracle, but the next paper was extremely difficult. I could not make anything work, and the publisher came by my desk at one point and, in exasperation said, "Just do *something* for God's sake. We are going to press in a few hours." After that, I had a long journey to get back respect from the staff. They criticized my editorial articles, my writing style and everything else I did, but the owners loved me. In six months, I had them in the black. A year later, they closed the paper and put the entire building, complete with printing presses, on the market.

My journey then took me back to my little town after the president of the Chamber of Commerce approached me about starting my own newspaper. He was convinced the town would support it with their advertising. I had some gold coins I had purchased years back as an investment and I looked into a new Apple product called desktop publishing. I was invited to speak at the Chamber's Christmas dinner and there I made my appeal to the members that I needed their support if I was to gamble on publishing my own paper.

My first edition took three weeks to get ready for the presses. I set up shop in our hobby room off the garage. I sold all the ads and wrote all the copy. I had hired a "composition" gal to help me make up the ads and put the paper together. We learned how to navigate around the computer together. Thank God for user-friendly MAC. I vowed to distribute the paper to every postal customer in our area and keep my circulation numbers up.

Soon, I was able to rent office space in town. I hired a reporter from the large syndicated county paper and, between the two of us, we tried to expose any corruption by county officials. Some were consequently voted out of office or run out of the country. I understand one man in the Savings and Loan Industry is still in South America. We found ordinary people in the county who were accomplishing good things and published their causes. We placed a scripture or good word for the day on every front page. I wrote an uplifting, encouraging editorial in every edition and we were considered a "good news" newspaper. We were definitely a blessing in the community.

It came to my attention about a local police matter involving a local African American family. Their son was on death row and all appeals had been exhausted. They believed he had been railroaded ten years earlier in a murder trial. My editor and I drove up to the prison and interviewed the young man. We decided to look into the case and caused a big commotion at the police department. Evidence had gone missing from the courthouse and police records were covered in White-Out, the stuff used to cover typos in those days. We shared everything we found with our readers and soon, he was awarded a new trial in another county and consequently acquitted of murder.

There is one major thing I learned from this episode in my life. When we surrender our life to God and follow through with trust, we can expect to be guided into situations outside the norm and these possibly bordering on the dangerous. I was exposing some important people in the community who at the very least were guilty of incompetence. Had I not been convinced of God's guiding hand, I would not have had the courage to publish the things I did.

As you and others accept your ability to facilitate miracles in our world, the less we will see of the injustices that now abound. That young man who is now free certainly believes in miracles.

Chapter 12
Step Up and Do It

"Just as there is no loss of basic energy in the universe, so no thought or action is without its effects, present or ultimate, seen or unseen, felt or unfelt."
~ Norman Cousins (1912-1990)

I know we laugh about TV evangelists who step up to microphones when storms threaten their shores and claim to turn away hurricanes. But there is something valid in our ability as spiritually connected beings to have authority over weather, and Jesus set the example for us. He used divine power (intention, expectation?) to calm the wind and sea and we can, too—if we believe enough. Here is an account from our not too distant history when prayers for help from weather conditions were dramatically answered.

Beatrice Schuller

DUNKIRK. In June 1940, 400,000 British and French soldiers were trapped on the north coast of France at Dunkirk. The Nazi forces were only ten miles away and could have cornered Allied troops. However, at this time, thick fog and clouds settled over the beaches. The English Channel also became unusually calm, and many small boats from England were able to ferry soldiers across to safety. The protective weather pattern lasted nine days while the men were evacuated. The Allied army was thus preserved to fight another day. Winston Churchill called the evacuation of Dunkirk a "miracle of deliverance."

Now, I will share from my own experience in the late 90s in Houston, when Robert, my husband of thirty years, was in hospital for some light surgery. He had received preliminary anesthesia as we waited in his room. There was a TV monitor on the wall and the weather channel was broadcasting information on the hurricane sitting stalled in the middle of the Gulf of Mexico, just to the east of Galveston and Houston. My eye caught a strange sight out the window to the side of the TV. A limp wind sock on top of the high-rise next door began to pick up air and blow to the west. A little later, the weather station was reporting on the movement of the hurricane due West right into the Houston area. The wind sock now was sticking straight out to the west. The door opened and Robert was wheeled out. I followed him to the surgical room, kissed him, and hurried back to the room.

My eyes fell on that wind sock again and I found myself speaking out to the winds themselves, something like, "Oh, wind of the west and the north. I ask you to come forth and send this storm south and dissipate it. Come forth and guide it to where no one will be hurt. I command you to come forth winds of the west and north." I kind of felt uncomfortable, like I was an actress on a stage or in a movie, but I persevered anyway.

Yes, I felt a little silly but, more than that, I felt God was pleased at what I was doing. I watched the wind sock while making my demands and a big smile crept across my face as I saw the wind sock start turning until the winds were blowing to the south. It wasn't too long before the weatherman was reporting on the new direction of the storm, noting that strong winds out of the northwest were moving the storm to the south. The storm had weakened significantly when it finally made landfall below Texas in an uninhabited coastal area of Mexico. I was elated and astounded at the same time.

The next tangle I had with weather was years later after Robert had suffered a fatal heart attack in our home. We had mortgaged our property to put in an RV park. It was to be a means to retire and spend our lives together on the land and in our beautiful home. His sudden death placed me in a position to get that park in and partially filled before the payments on the note became due. I made funeral arrangements in shock, carried along by an unseen power, as most of us do when losing loved ones. I had no time to mourn and actually had to fire the general contractor the day of Robert's funeral. The guy met me and my sons as we arrived at the property. He stopped us on the driveway and demanded I advance him more money immediately or he would park his dozer on the wet slab just poured for the office.

I find it very difficult to return to that time of darkness after my husband's death. As I have learned to practice living in the present and worked to heal old wounds, it is almost as if it never happened. My survival—physically and financially— was in jeopardy, and I would struggle through the darkness, unable to see a light at the end, though convinced my faithful companion still held my hand. I suppose you could compare it to that beautiful song, "You'll Never Walk Alone."

In many ways, my children tried to help me through the challenges as best they could, but most of my choices created a chasm between us too deep to cross. We would suffer through this estrangement for several years before family bonds were restored. Our focus on healing and forgiveness has now borne fruit and resulted in respectful loving relationships.

Through a multitude of divine interventions that took me to 2005, the park was completed and a few permanent campers were scattered throughout the sites. Several RV clubs were holding rallies in the park, and business was picking up. I had saved many of the tall hardwood trees, and all utilities were underground. It was a beautiful ten-acre park with a stocked pond for fishing and I had two little paddle boats.

On this particular day, there was a dozen or so weekly and daily trailers on site along with several large motor homes and some Fifth wheels nestled under the beautiful trees.

I had seen weather forecasts the night before for thunderstorms and it was already clouding up as I opened up the office. My usual early risers were sitting out front having coffee and June, my part time helper, followed me inside. She turned on the computer monitor while I turned on the TV. I gasped at the long uninterrupted line of thunderstorms stretching the entire length of the county. The radar picture on the monitor was showing an ominous solid red area heading right for us. The TV was reporting on a tornado sighted on the ground to the southwest of us.

I ran back outside and looked around at dark clouds overhead and around the park in every direction I turned. Then a cool wind began whipping my hair across my face. I turned and asked the campers to secure the empty chairs up under the porch. As I looked up at the sky, a large drop of rain splattered on my forehead and then another one hit me in the eye.

I looked up into the sky and heard myself crying out, "MERCY—I CRY FOR MERCY AND PROTECTION FROM THIS STORM FOR ME AND ALL THESE CAMPERS!"

I stood on the walkway to the office and raised my arms and hands to the sky. There was a distant rumble of thunder that seemed to go on forever.

"MERCY, I DECLARE MERCY FROM THESE WINDS AND LIGHTNING!"

I heard one of the men in back say, "You trying to control the weather now, Beatrice?"

They all snickered. Then I waited. There was no more raindrops hitting me and the wind stilled. I opened my eyes and saw blue sky above, but the wall of gray still engulfed the entire area in all directions. I ran back inside to look at the monitor and couldn't believe my eyes. There was a little circle outlined in the middle of all that red and I knew we were safely inside it. A tornado damaged some homes and uprooted trees one-half mile from the park, but no one was hurt and I could hardly contain the gratitude I felt in my heart for the storm bypassing us.

Do you see what a wonderful Source of love and power we all have if only we would have the courage to step into it? Belief and the accompanying expectation are powerful elements that you can use to facilitate your own miracles. Please don't start thinking you're not "spiritual" enough or "trained in healing," or brought up in church, or any other reason.

I think of Moses raised in a dynasty of Egyptian rule but when called to lead the Israelites out of slavery, he had no faith in himself for the task. When he asked who he was supposed to say sent him, he was told, "Say I AM sent you." This was the great message we take away: Labels do not define who God is. He is the Source of All that is. If you choose to believe, then you are one with God. Jesus did and Mother Teresa did, and Nelson Mandela did and Martin Luther King did, and millions of everyday people down through the ages. They all connected with and facilitated the One they trusted and—miracles followed.

There are multitudes of good people who accomplish a lot of good things even though they are not awakened to the Divine one within them. Perhaps you are one of the happy well-adjusted people, raised by good and stable parents who naturally know you are loved. You respect yourself and take good care of mind and body. You are a good role model. Thank God there are lots of you out there who have blessed our world with your efforts and achievements. But even high achievers can benefit from the knowledge and understanding of facilitating a miracle.

Chapter 13
I Left My Heart...

Your function on earth is healing.
~ A Course in Miracles (Text 12,Vii,4)

My latest miracle happened here in Sedona in 2014 when I received a brand new heart. Because of all the stress in my life after my husband's death, I suffered two heart attacks and received seven stents between 2000 and 2010.

The invention of stents is a miracle in itself and has saved millions of lives. After the last surgery in 2010, the doctor told my son, "God must have some reason for your mother to be here because with that blockage, she shouldn't be alive." I moved to this high altitude in Sedona from the Texas Coast about two years ago and hiked all over the red rocks without a problem. Nevertheless, two

months ago upon impulse while attending a Unity
fellowship meeting, I felt led to ask one of the
chaplains to pray with me. I told her I was seeking
wisdom for taking care of my heart and staying
healthy. This young woman stood behind me,
praying silently as I sat in a chair. I was also
praying in silence when I "heard" the Divine voice
within; "I am giving you a new heart." I thanked
the lady for her help without disclosing what I had
heard, although I would later share it with her. And
so I went home very excited about receiving my
new heart.

A few weeks later, I began having chest pains
and after three days and nights with no relief and
accompanied with much praying, I appeased my
husband and went in to see a cardiologist. With my
history, he did not hesitate to admit me to the
hospital immediately to perform an angiogram.
This is the procedure where they put a probe in
your artery and release a dye around your heart to
expose any blockages you may have.

After the procedure, the doctor told me he could
not find anything to fix and I asked him about the
damage on the bottom of my heart. "There is no
damage to your heart," he said. I then asked what
my heart looked like. "Your heart is beautiful," he
said with a warm smile. He told me I could pick up
the disk and watch the procedure for myself. Later

that week, my husband and I watched the disk and were reassured to see the blood pumping all the way to the bottom of my heart where it previously had been dark. Since receiving my new heart, my cardiologist has taken me off two drugs with potentially harmful side effects. I no longer need statins and Plavix, a blood thinner.

And so we return full circle to trusting and then obeying and expecting. In the physical world, "Seeing is believing," but in the world of miracles, we know and believe first and then "It is." Here we have another example of trusting first and then following the guidance we are given, sometimes intuitively and sometimes prompted by outside sources.

I did not scoff at the idea of a new heart, although it seemed impossible at the time. At this point in my life, I can honestly say I do believe that with God, all things are possible. With my track record, I would have to be slightly nuts to believe otherwise. I hope your faith in possibilities has been increased through the sharing of these miraculous events in my life. I would not recommend taking yourself off any medications without the consent of your doctor who is treating you. There are obviously times when we must depend on these medications until we may get to a place where they are no longer needed.

Keep in mind that our mortal lives are complex exercises on Earth— much like a schoolhouse. Some of us need a lifetime of learning in the "school of hard knocks," as they say. Others have it pretty easy for most of their lives.

Chapter 14
Darth Vader Back When

"For what is Mysticism? Is it not the attempt to draw near to God, not by rites or ceremonies, but by inward disposition? Is it not merely a hard word for 'The Kingdom of Heaven is within'? Heaven is neither a place nor a time."

~ Florence Nightingale (1820-1910)

There are other types of unusual occurrences that may or may not be considered miraculous, and I like to label them as "paranormal." Webster's definition of that term is "beyond normal explanation; supernatural."

Wikipedia describes *paranormal* as: A general term that designates experiences that lie outside "the range of normal experience or scientific explanation or that indicates phenomena understood to be outside of science's current ability to explain or measure…."

This first incident occurred after I was struck by lightning as a child, which I related earlier. Return with me to the Christmas after the summer lightening strike. Santa had brought a tricycle and I was riding from one room to another trying to master the mechanics of turning around. I would head to the kitchen from the living room at Grandmother's house, pedal through the dining room and then enter the darkened kitchen, and try to maneuver into a turn in front of the refrigerator. The kitchen light was not on, but a big floodlight outside the window afforded me enough light to see where to turn around and head back into the brightly lit living room. I remember all this as if it were yesterday, seeing it through those three-year-old eyes. On about my third turn at the fridge, I had to rise off the seat and turn the tricycle around. Some movement caught my eye at the row of kitchen windows, located high up on the wall above and adjacent to the cooking stove. There stood a tall "Darth Vader"-looking figure. I could not make out a face within the black hood but I could see the eyes, and they were staring right into mine. The hood came down to broad shoulders and a closed black cloak. This creature was clearly lit by the security light attached near the window and under the eave of the roof.

I was paralyzed by a feeling of stark terror and gripped the handles of my tricycle as my eyes stayed locked onto that creature. Finally, I was able to find my voice and gave out an ear-splitting scream. Everyone came running from the living room and my daddy scooped me up into his arms. Someone turned on the light. I was shaking from fear and looked gratefully into the face of my daddy.

"What happened, baby?" he asked.

He was looking over my body and my mother was checking me out as well. Stuttering and shaking, I finally was able to tell them what I had seen, calling it a "big black monster" outside in the light. I refused to look at that window and clung tightly to my daddy. He continued to calm me down and, after transferring me to my mother's arms, he went outside as promised and looked around. He returned and told us he saw no one outside.

Several days later, I was in town with my mother when a large delivery truck pulled up alongside the sidewalk. It was painted solid black. I couldn't take my eyes off it and then—nothing.

Mother explained later that I went into what she called a "convulsion," a condition where your eyes roll back into your head and your whole body goes into a spasm and you are in danger of swallowing your tongue and choking or biting off your tongue. I continued to have these seizures every time I saw any large black object. Of course, I was taken to doctors, but none of them could find a cause for the "fits."

I remember one such visit sitting in front of the doctor's desk and him suggesting that I may be faking the seizures. My daddy jumped up and grabbed the doctor by the collar and called him a bad word. How a doctor could believe a little girl could fake foaming at the mouth and biting her own tongue is hard to believe.

This situation went on for several months until someone suggested Mother drive me seventy-five miles away to take me to a chiropractor husband/wife team. I believe Mother drove me to their clinic several times. I never had another seizure and I remember how they would remove my little sandals and give them to Mother while I went back to the treatment room with them. There on their big table, they would push around on my neck and back very gently and speak in whispers. Then while the lady doctor helped me on with my dress, the other doctor talked with Mother.

Maybe they were doing what those in the metaphysical field today call "energy work." This is an effective way to release any obstructions we may be carrying that hinders our living a healthy and productive life. You could call it New Age deliverance I suppose. At any rate, I never had a problem with seeing black images again. Whatever the source of that malady, I was delivered and never suffered another seizure.

In the event you witness something in this realm, I would want you to maintain a healthy perception of what you are seeing. Many times, I have warded off any uncomfortable feelings when witnessing a paranormal event by recalling a scripture:[12] "For God has not given us a spirit of fear, but of power and love and a sound mind." Remember, you are *at one* with an eternal Divine Being while having a physical experience on this planet. We know from Biblical recordings that Jesus had total authority over any dark forces he confronted while here on Earth. We share in that authority as children (sons) of God.

---

[12] Eph. 2:8

Chapter 15

Encounters of
the Weird Kind

"Those things that nature denied to human sight, she revealed to the eyes of the soul."

~ Ovid (43 BC - AD 17)

One of my favorite paranormal experiences involved what are called the Marfa lights outside a tiny town in West Texas. Many people drive there hoping to see the lights that only rarely appear. They have been seen there off and on ever since the little community was established in the 1800s. I ended up there when I took my mother and mother-in-law on a road trip to see 'Big Bend," a mountainous area on the Mexican border.

We arrived in Ft. Davis and settled in to our motel room and then headed south before sunset to see if the lights would show themselves. We had spent some time earlier reading of the history of these mysterious lights. At one time, a group had taken jeeps out and, when the lights appeared, they would drive straight through them as they danced around or went off and on as they were reported to do. That was not so surprising when you consider that a beam of light is not a solid thing you can grasp or pick up and put in a box. Still, there was no scientific explanation as to how or why the lights appeared at times.

As we stood outside the tall chain-link fence of the parking area on the side of the highway, I peered out at the expanse of low shrubs and cacti below a rise of hills about two football fields away, waiting as the sun dropped below the horizon. Immediately the lights appeared, first one and then another, and then a set of three moving together.

Once, a red light appeared and moved around. It was great fun to watch and as it grew darker, I noticed some very small lights appearing in the brush close to the fence about twenty feet out or so. I pointed them out to other people there and we were amazed as we watched the lights coming closer, appearing and then quickly disappearing, only to appear in a nearby bush.

Then when there was only a faint lightness left from the sun on the far horizon, I noticed a tiny light just on the other side of the tall fence just seeming to hang in the air. I walked over and got as close to the fence as I could, completely in awe with a sense that the light and I were communicating on some level.

I heard my mother approaching. I told her to look at the light that had come over to us. She laughed.

"Beatrice—that is not one of the lights. It is just sunlight reflected from Venus shining on the horizon."

All of a sudden, we saw the light start moving away and then it shot away and disappeared before our very eyes. I turned to mother, "I guess we just lost Venus," We both laughed. We then heard thunder and saw clouds filled with lightning back towards Ft. Davis and the road we had driven down. We hurried to the car and drove into a lightning storm more severe than any of us had ever witnessed. We couldn't even talk, it was so loud with only seconds between the ear-splitting claps. There was not a drop of rain and the lightning could be seen coming up out of the ground all around us. As soon as we entered town, the rain began and, thankfully, the lightning and thunder ended. We took refuge in our room, grateful for the normal sound of a gentle rain.

I visited Marfa two more times over the years and, both times, the lights appeared and put on a show, coming right up to the fence. The last time, the county had installed a covered bleacher for viewing, and other travelers watched the lights with me. My friend John (whom later would become my husband) was with me then and he video taped the lights.

A very different experience with light beings occurred on the dairy farm in January 1995. My widowed mother had suffered a stroke and I and other family members had driven down to see her in the hospital. We returned to Mother's house near midnight. Soon I was climbing into her bed piled high with quilts. I prayed for Mother and all of us gathered there. It was near freezing and I could hear the wind still blowing the drizzling rain against the window next to the bed. After a few minutes, I could see a star twinkling between the closed blinds. Soon, there were three more twinkling lights. *Strange, I thought. The weather must be clearing.* I got up and peeked through the blind. I couldn't believe my eyes. I yanked the cord, raising the entire blind all the way to the top. Pressing my nose against the cold window, I stared in wonder at the forty-foot eucalyptus tree standing about 8 feet from the house. Dozens of golden lights, a little larger than standard white

Christmas lights, were vibrating in erratic little circles. Their movements left a glowing tail like a "sparkler" when it is twirled around. The lights were scattered among the tree, moving with the branches in the wind.

As I watched, I realized they were increasing in number, but none were flying to the tree, they just appeared and joined the rest of the group. I left the room and went to wake my sister but she was out like a light and I could not awaken her even though I shook her shoulder and called her name. Next I went to her son and woke him up. He was groggy, too, but I told him about the lights and asked him if he ever heard of lightning bugs that never blink off. My mind was trying to come up with a logical explanation. "I don't know, Aunt Bea," he said, and fell back to sleep. I then went to the windows in every room peering outside into the pitch-black darkness but I did not see a single light.

I returned to the bedroom and now there were so many lights in the tree that the ground was lit up all around it. My thought was that anyone driving by on the county road would think we had strung hundreds of Christmas lights in the tree. I could not take my eyes off those lights and lay there watching them. The last time I remember looking at the clock, it was 3:00 a.m.

The next morning, I examined the tree and found no sign of anything unusual. As I related the strange incident at breakfast, my sister was very blasé, suggesting I had dreamed it. Her son spoke up and told her how I had woken him up and asked about them. My husband later assured me it could not have been any insect with the near-freezing temperatures and rain that time of year.

Now I know that light beings exist and think it plausible they gather energy from things here on Earth like lightning or other sources. Maybe someday we can communicate with them on some level. I will never forget the ones who watched over me and my mother that night. She was able to talk with me next morning and eventually made a full recovery from the effects of the stroke. We should never take our prayers and thoughts for granted. They can be very powerful and effective. When I prayed that night after lying down in bed, I had no idea I was calling in protective beings of light. It was many years before I figured out what those lights really were and could finally put my curiosity to rest.

Conclusion

"The book of Proverbs (23:7) proclaims, 'As a man thinketh in his heart so is he.' This adage reaches out to every condition and circumstance of human endeavor. Each of us is literally 'what we think,' and our character being the complete sum of all our thoughts."

~ James Allen

I am grateful to have this opportunity to share what I have learned through my own experiences about the reality of modern-day miracles. If you have surrendered your life to God (by any other name or label), then you are already facilitating miracles and the world is blessed. If you have not yet awakened to the reality of your Divine origin, I urge you to take a leap of faith and just ask for the experience. We are all loved unconditionally and can reunite with our Creator. The sooner we realize we are all connected to the same Source of All That

Is and therefore to one another, the sooner we can facilitate a miraculous transformation of ourselves, our nations, and our planet.

The components for facilitating miracles revealed in this book have proven effective time and again throughout my life as these experiences demonstrate. God's will for all is love, joy, peace, and abundance. If that is the outcome for all concerned in a situation, then it is safe to anticipate and trust a response and then take action as directed. If you lack faith to believe in such a loving, powerful God, ask for more faith. Your request will surely be heard and who knows what adventure you may experience in order to receive a bountiful supply of faith.

I met the Spirit Parent by way of Jesus Christ who introduced me to another aspect of Father God, the Holy Spirit who then became my teacher. I can tell you that the God of Unconditional Love will appear to each of us in the way most receptive according to our culture or beliefs. The Greek meaning for Christ is "anointed one."[13] Jesus of Nazareth was an anointed Son of God. He knew his life purpose at an early age and set about explaining that He and all of us were children of a heavenly "Father." Many great prophets and spiritual giants have devoted their lives to the Divine Father.

---

[13] Strong's # 5547 NAS Greek Lexicon

These mysterious happenings I have related should be recognized for what they are: evidence of our unity with one another and alignment with the Creator. Now we are beginning to understand that we are all connected and we will be experiencing even greater things as we manifest God. My hope and prayer is that you have your own experience of connecting with that Divine One within and begin to facilitate your own miracles.

For those of you (and there are multitudes out there) who are already living a life of miracles, I encourage you to share what you know to be true with those who cross your path. Let us access that seat of power within and join forces to create the heaven on Earth we all seek.

Peace, love, joy, and abundance to all my brothers and sisters in every nation on this beautiful planet. Connecting with one another in a spirit of love is available to us all and will change ourselves and therefore our world. Included below are affirmations that were shared with me and I pass them along to you. I know you will surely find some of your own to empower your thoughts as you go through your own incredible journey.

I would love to hear from you. Feel free to visit my website/blog and leave any questions or comments you may have: www.beatriceschuller.com.

Something To Share

Whatever you want to be, start to develop that pattern now. You can instill any trend in your consciousness right now, provided you inject a strong thought in your mind; then your actions and whole being will obey that thought.

~ Paramahansa Yogananda

B ecause of my background that I reluctantly included in this book, it was difficult, if not impossible, for me to get to the place of manifesting God and facilitating miracles without understanding who I truly was. The miraculous encounter with the Spirit in 1974 after my desperate plea for help was the first time I understood I was truly a child of God. The unspeakable joy that flowed through me was proof of that divine love. I was family and I was being rescued from my own destructive nature.

Next came a renewing of my mind by replacing all the false beliefs about myself with the truth. I was not a hopelessly depressed woman powerless to break her shameful behavior and feelings of inferiority. I had a miracle working "Go-To Source."

This process was accelerated four years ago after I joined a Louise Hay Cruise featuring Dr. Wayne Dyer and other speakers who encouraged me to continually mind my thoughts and words. I was a work in progress of learning the way to peace, love, joy, and abundance.

Then, two years ago, I was encouraged to make it a moment-by-moment practice as needed. I put this practice to work with the aid of an internet friend, a fellow author who shared some of his mind-changing affirmations with me. I want to share them with you, and, if they help you, then you can pass the process forward to others.[14]

I have memorized these statements and start my day with them. Thereafter throughout the day and night as soon as I become aware of thoughts of darkness or false beliefs, I gratefully and joyously replace them with these empowering truths:

I am in and of the will of God. I want and have nothing else and no other thought or feeling shall have a permanent place in me. I AM.

---

[14] www.spiritualhealingsource.com-Brad Cullen

I choose to live and I release stress, tension, and resistance and the origins and memories of them from wherever they are stored. Every part of this body I occupy, consciously or unconsciously, is being brought into alignment with the Creator of the Universe and everything in it. I am being guided and directed into oneness with Infinite Creation, thus I am moving into all things and substance beyond the ability of my finite mind to achieve, yet my finite mind is being energized to be and now is an instrument for the Divine. This body is now stress and tension-free and therefore in perfect health and peace.

I extend love and forgiveness to all and bring about integration of everything past, present, and future. Every day in every way I am getting better, better and better.

www.ingramcontent.com/pod-product-compliance
Lightning Source LLC
Chambersburg PA
CBHW031552040426
42452CB00006B/281